Usha M[...]
Vegetarian Kitchen

Low-fat Epicurean Delights

by

Usha Meister

Usha Meister's Vegetarian Kitchen
by Usha Meister

Published by Usha Meister & Associates
First Printing, September 1996
Second Printing, January 1997

Canadian Cataloguing in Publication Data

Meister, Usha, 1952-
Usha Meister's Vegetarian Kitchen

Includes index.
ISBN 0-9681142-0-2

1. Vegetarian cookery.   2. Low-fat diet - Recipes.
I. Title.   II. Title: Vegetarian Kitchen.

TX837.M44   1996   641.5'636 C96-931610-0

Photographs by : Bob Chambers Photography, Burlington, Canada

Cartoons by : Andy Kefford, Hamilton, Canada

Printed in Canada by :   **CASCADE PRINTING**
Niagara Falls, Canada

Dedicated to
my loving husband Chuck, my Herculean
pillar, for his selfless love....
&
my lovely daughter, Divya, who is always in
my heart....

Special thanks to :

My parents, for their loving encouragement and teaching me how to be economical while achieving what you want in life.

Chuck, for being my "sous chef" and always having a kind word for the food I put in front of him, saying " It's Tasty ". What would I do without those encouraging words !!

Divya, my daughter, who at age 2, gave me my very first compliment about how good I cook and how she wanted to own her own cooking school.

Pearl, my mother-in-law, who encourages me to pursue my dreams and gets jittery everytime I contemplate returning to the field of computers.

Cisco Mancini, for being my right hand woman and being there whenever I needed her, for reviewing and tasting recipes, help in cooking, for some of her accessories for the food photography. The list goes on....

Marilu Disanto, my nutrition consultant, for her invaluable help especially in the analysis of the recipes.

Patricia Charney, for always being there with her positive comments, for reviewing my recipes and for some of her accessories for the food photography.

Arnold Rose, my editor Emeritus, who went through this book with a fine tooth comb.

Gloria Mostyn, for reviewing the recipes and all other help.

Brent Whitton, my youngest student, for testing some of the recipes.

Suzanne Bourret, The Hamilton Spectator, Food and Restaurant writer, for all her support over the years, giving me timely publicity and fabulous articles.

Susan Bowinkelman, Program Manager, Mohawk College, for believing in my foresight about low-fat cooking courses, and helping me promote those courses.

Rob Sheppard, of Rogers Cable, for giving me my first break in television .

Thanks to Lawrence Diskin, Dan McLean, Connie Smith and the crew at CHCH 11, "News at Noon", for their professionalism and making my T.V. appearances so much fun.

My siblings, Uma, Udya, Latha & Bala for being my primary motivators and saying that they just loved whatever I cooked. My brother Bala for devouring whatever was put in front of him.

My brothers-in-law, sister-in-law and my numerous nieces and nephews, for the enthusiasm shown in my cooking pursuits and in my food.

My numerous students and friends, especially Arie & Joanna Vanderspek, Joanna & Frank Christennson, Bert Rosnick, Ursula Goodman, Irene Bettoil & Diane Sandler, who always have an encouraging word for me.

My list can go on and on...................... My heartfelt thanks to you all.

Table of Contents

Foreword

RIDING THE VEGGIE HIGHWAY

Hors d'oeuvres

Dips, Sauces & Chutneys

Tropical Salsa Cruda, 36
Decadent Date Chutney, 37
Cheese and Chives Dip, 38
Velvety Vanilla Yogurt Dip, 39
Fruit Raita, 39
Herbed Bean Paté, 40
Homemade Relish, 41
Verdant Pesto, 41
Taratour Sauce, 42
Tzaziki, 42

Hearty Soups

Cajun Corn Soup, 44
Potato and Barley Soup, 45
Dry Vegetable Broth Mix, 46
Cabbage and Potato Soup, 47
Potaje Murciano, 48
Tomato Rasam, 49
Pasta E Fagioli, 51
Manchurian Soup, 53
Vegetable Dal, 55
Sweet Corn Soup, 56

Salads & Dressings

Carrapple Slaw, 58
The McBean Salad, 59
Rojak (Malaysian Salad), 60
Andalusian Salad, 61
Fattoush, 63
Bulgur & Chick Pea Salad, 64
Herculean Greek Salad, 65
Spinach and Orange Salad, 66
Tropical Salad, 67

Andalusian Dressing, 68
Calypso Salad Dressing, 68
Greek Salad Dressing, 69
Middle-Eastern Salad Dressing, 69
Poppy Seed Dressing, 70
Lebanese Dressing, 70
Malaysian Dressing, 71
Mexican Dressing, 71
Coleslaw Dressing, 72

Rice , Pasta & One Dish Meals

Mexican Rice, 74
Masala Khichari (Rice & Lentil Pilaf), 75
Vegetable Biryani (Vegetable Fried Rice), 77
David's High Energy Lasagna, 79
Athenian Pie, 81
Pad Thai, 83
Veggie Loaf or Veggie Patties, 85
Kasha & Potato Crust Quiche, 87
Volcanic Enchiladas, 89
Aztec Corn Casserole, 91
Broccoli Risotto Torte with Tomato Sauce, 93
Usha's Upma (Cream of Wheat Pilaf), 95
Szechwan Rice, 97
Vegetarian Paella, 98

Vegetable Ecstasies

Harvest Ratatouille, 100
Mathan Patchadi (Squash Curry), 101
Alu Gobi (Potato & Cauliflower Curry), 103
Bhaingan Bhartha (Eggplant Dip), 104

Muffins, Breads, Flatbreads & Cakes

Foreword by

Kim.L.Ireland, H.B.Sc., M.D, Family Medicine, Hamilton, Ontario

I was both flattered and excited when Usha asked me if I would like to write the foreword for her first cookbook. This book responds to the desire for a healthy life that many people in our society feel.

The evidence is overwhelming that the recipe for general personal health and quality of life can be enhanced through a few key ingredients. These ingredients include regular exercise, avoiding bad habits such as smoking, managing stress, and of course, what many find most challenging: eating healthy food. Most people know that vegetables, fruits and legumes are good for them, and that saturated fat and cholesterol are bad for them. The problem is finding tasty recipes that fulfill these requirements and developing the skills to prepare such recipes.

This is where Usha comes in. She has created, in this book, a gold mine of stunning recipes that will amaze you with their variety of flavors, aromas and easily available ingredients. The wonderful part is that all of these recipes are good for you. But you don't have to take my word for it. Just check the nutrition analysis that appears at the end of each recipe. There are exotic, but lean recipes here that will please every member of the family. Usha covers just about every major international cuisine in this volume. Once you have gotten used to these exciting low-fat dishes, you'll wonder how you ever, in the past, settled for meat and potatoes. I guarantee, you will never again end up scratching your head and wondering what to make for dinner. Usha will always come to your aid.

Usha has written these recipes in a clear, easy-to-follow, highly readable manner. Each step is laid out for you in a way that is manageable for even the most hesitant cook. In fact, the book is reflective of the personality of the Usha I know: straightforward and reliable. In no time at all, you will look forward to cooking and feel like an expert in the kitchen. Just let Usha guide you. She has produced a book that you will use over and over again. This book is meant to be enjoyed by you and recommended to or given as a gift to friends and relatives. You see, you will not be giving just a book, but the gift of health to people you care about.

Through this book, Usha is sharing her vast knowledge of low-fat vegetarian world cuisine. In this respect, she is in the vanguard of those who are contributing to something besides good food that as a doctor, I can appreciate: Preventative medicine.

Dear Reader,

Since my earliest years, in India, I have had a fascination with cooking. As a child, I would secretly cook in the kitchen whenever my parents had gone out for the evening. This helped me to master the fundamentals of cooking - speed, economy of ingredients and innovation. I would prepare recipes I liked and they had to be consumed by my sisters and brother before my parents returned. Once they discovered my secret passion, my parents assured me I could cook whatever I wished, but they had to be there to monitor me (fire hazard) in case I needed help. My parents, especially my father, always gave me free reign in the kitchen, thereby making it possible for me to cook exotic food, even in difficult times. I thank them from the bottom of my heart for the encouragement given to me over those years.

Then there was the period when my cooking skills were used as a benchmark by my relatives. They always looked forward to my cooking and soon I became the standard bearer to whom all others were compared. "Does she/he cook better than Usha?", was the inevitable question. At a young age, I used to delight at the thought of teaching someone how to cook. I started collecting recipes early on and if I found someone with a new recipe, I found ways of becoming their friend.

Those formative years passed quickly. Necessity always made me come up with recipes and when I could not find the right ingredients or kitchen utensils to cook with, I used to make do with whatever was available. In those innocent times, eating HEALTHY food was never a concern. But my cooking evolved with the passage of time. I moved away from traditional fat-laden recipes and quickly learnt the art of creating the low-fat variety.

My daughter Divya, who loves cooking as much as I do, soon became a fan of my special skills. At age 2, she used to park herself on a chair in the kitchen and constantly ask me "What are you doing now?". I had to give her a detailed description. Though she was too young to fully understand my explanations, she would nod her head enthusiastically. At the age of 8, she prepared a complete meal, using the microwave oven. It was then that I realized that if I could teach a child that young, I could teach anyone.

During my travels all over the world, I was impressed by the way the inhabitants of each country used the ingredients available to them to come up with different dishes. Unfortunately, my enthusiasm for all these different culinary achievements led to self-indulgence. The results started showing on my body and I realized that, even though I was a vegetarian, too much of any good thing can be bad for you.

Here in Canada, I have seen a lot of my friends fall victim to yo-yo dieting. They battle a weight problem in a variety of ways, succumbing to the latest weight loss fads. One particular group of friends would tell me every time I saw them that they had each lost 10 lb. on a salad diet or fruit juice diet. But within 6 months they always gained back their original weight.

I was disturbed by what I saw around me and frustrated with the way I was juggling my own diet. It was then I decided that I had to do something about it.

About this time, I met Chuck, my future husband. Four mutual interests attracted us to each other -- our love for singer Tom Jones, the Welsh international super-star; English Literature, Psychology and ...... our great love for good food ! Chuck introduced me to western ideas of exercising the mind and the body and I introduced him to my eastern thought and exotic dishes. Together the two of us were determined to take control of our bodies.

We joined a health club, started doing weight training coupled with cardio exercise. These days, we have no dietary restrictions (except

11

following a low-fat diet) and we make sure we read all the labels on store bought items (checking for fat content). Weight gain no longer seems to be a problem, now that we have changed our life-style and consistently maintain those changes .

I had to revise my entire database and restrict its contents to ultra low-fat recipes. About this time, I introduced my first low-fat cooking course, "Cooking the Light Hearted way", at Mohawk College, Hamilton, Canada.

The recipes in this book have been tested over the last 7 years and have undergone substantial modifications to accommodate different requests. I am proud to say that each new course and new recipe introduced by me has met with resounding success and applause. My loyal students call me "the guru of low-fat vegetarian cooking".

In 1994, I opened Usha Meister's "School of Vegetarian Cooking". Friends who thought I was crazy to teach "Low-fat Vegetarian" soon became avid fans and have slowly learned to substitute my low-fat recipes for their former " meat and potato " diet.

Some of my students are angina and stroke victims. They thank me profusely for teaching them the techniques involved in low-fat cooking and also for introducing them to a variety of cuisine's, all prepared the low-fat way. Their expressions of appreciation are extremely rewarding for me as I feel I have contributed towards their well-being.

In this book, you will find recipes which I use on a daily basis. My students and friends all use them and I hope that you will enjoy them too. I am happy that the release of my book coincides with two birthdays, my daughter Divya's 18th birthday and the sesquicentennial (150 years) celebrations of Hamilton, Canada.

Happy cooking and Bon Appetit !

Culinary tips from the "Low-Fat" food Meister

- Never add salt to beans or lentils when cooking them.
- Lentils and beans take much longer to cook in an acidic base (e.g.: tomatoes, lemon juice, tamarind etc..) .
- Always add the salt last when cooking beans.
- Before using canned Beans in a recipe, rinse them clean under running water (this removes the added salt and brine it was sitting in) , and use as required.
- Large dried beans need to be soaked for 6-8 hours, depending on their size, prior to cooking them (e.g: chick peas, red or white kidney beans, black-eyed beans, lima beans, etc.).
- Rinse the soaked raw beans clean before cooking. This helps reduce flatulence.
- Lentils require only 1/2 hour of pre-soaking time, because of their size.
- Cooked beans freeze well. You can make a double batch to cut down on future preparation time.
- Beans and lentils have to be cooked until soft.
- Most beans by themselves are not a complete protein, hence they need to be combined with rice or pasta.
- If you are eating beans or lentils for the first time, try them in small amounts, for they are difficult to digest. Then gradually increase the quantity you prepare.
- Put 3-4 dry bay leaves in the containers in which you store your beans, lentils and grains. The bay leaves keep unwanted visitors at bay (e.g. weevils).
- Add a pinch of salt while sautéing onions. This helps carmelize the onions and also speeds up the cooking time of the onions.
- Always add ginger and garlic after the onions are cooked to stop them from burning.
- A key point to remember when using Herbs and Spices:
  - ♥ To release the flavor and the essential oils in spices they need to be added at the beginning of the cooking process.
  - ♥ Always add herbs at the very end of your cooking, to preserve their nutrients.

How to Cook Grains

Grain	Grain:liquid	Yield	Cooking time
Amaranth	1 : 3	3 cups	20-25 minutes
Barley	1 : 4	4 cups	45-50 minutes
Bulgur **	1 : 2	3 cups	15-20 minutes
Couscous **	1 : 1½	3 cups	5 minutes
Kasha (buckwheat)	1 : 3	3½ cups	15-20 minutes
Millet	1 : 2	3 cups	20-30 minutes
Quinoa***	1 : 2	3 cups	20-25 minutes
Wild rice	1 : 4	4 cups	45-50 minutes
Rice (brown)	1 : 2½	3½ cups	45-50 minutes
Rice (white)	1 : 2	3 cups	20 minutes
Rice (Basmati)	1 : 1½	3 cups	20-25 minutes
Wheat Berries	1 : 3½	3.cups	40-60 minutes

The above chart illustrates the grain to liquid ratio, quantity it yields, and the approximate cooking time using the medium of your choice. I use a pressure cooker to cook my beans and lentil, as it cuts down cooking time by half.

• **To cook most grains** : Bring the required liquid to a boil then stir in the grain (as per chart grain:liquid). Cover the pan tightly. Reduce the heat to low. Simmer and cook until all the liquid has been absorbed. Turn off the heat and let the pan stand, covered, for about 5 minutes. Fluff the grain with a fork to separate and use as required.

**To cook Bulgur and Couscous : Bring liquid to a boil. Add the bulgur or couscous. Stir. Remove from heat. Cover and set aside for specified time or until soft.

***To cook Quinoa : Quinoa, a complete protein and a nutritional powerhouse, can be found at your local bulk food or health food store. Refrigerate in airtight containers as it tends to go rancid. Quinoa has a bitter outer coating. So before cooking, rinse clean under running water and set to drain. Then toast in a deep, dry skillet over medium-high heat for 12-15 minutes, until you can hear the crackling or when a nutty aroma emanates from the toasted quinoa.

How to read my Recipes

The organization of this book is simple and designed with you, the reader, in mind. Certain parts of a recipe are bolded to make a point For example:

Take for example "The Volcanic Enchiladas" recipe on Page 89

"For the **Bean and Cheese Filling**
2 cups **cooked** red kidney beans, **cooled & mashed lightly**"

The word cooked has been bolded because it may not be obvious that the beans are to be cooked. The cooled and mashed have been bolded because if the beans are not cool they will be runny.

So you can see how the smallest miscue can ruin a great recipe.

Throughout the book you'll find tips and variations (ideas). I hope you find them useful.

About the Nutritional Information

Nutritional information is provided for each recipe (per serving) including the % of calories from fat. Nutritional content may vary depending on the specific brands or type of ingredients used. "Optional" ingredients (ingredients you may want to do without) have their breakdown given in brackets in the Nutrition Analysis.
Total fats, as well as the breakdown to saturated, monounsaturated, and polyunsaturated fats are given for each recipe. The fatty acids seldom add up exactly to the total. This is due to rounding and to the existence of small amounts of other fatty acid components that are not included in the basic three categories.

Important

My book is not intended as a recommendation for any specific diet, nor as a substitute for your doctor's advice. It's purpose is to show how, with a balanced approach to eating, you can enjoy low-fat foods made from fruits, vegetables, beans and grains,

Touring My Spice (Dry Spices) Cupboard:

Welcome to my spice cupboard. I buy my spices in small quantities and store them in airtight bottles, in a cool, dark place. You can photocopy this page to use as a shopping list when buying unfamiliar spices.

- ☐ Cumin seeds
- ☐ Coriander seeds
- ☐ Dry red chilies
- ☐ Asafetida (known as Hing in East-Indian grocery stores)
- ☐ Turmeric (known as Haldi in East-Indian grocery stores)
- ☐ Fenugreek seeds (known as Methi in East-Indian grocery stores)
- ☐ Thymol seeds (known as Ajwain in East-Indian grocery stores)
- ☐ Onion Seeds (known as Kaloanji in East-Indian grocery stores)
- ☐ Mustard seeds
- ☐ Paprika
- ☐ Mexican chili powder (a mix of paprika, cumin powder, oregano & sugar)
- ☐ Italian seasoning (a mix of thyme, rosemary, oregano, basil & marjoram)
- ☐ Garlic powder
- ☐ Onion powder
- ☐ Dill weed
- ☐ Rosemary
- ☐ Basil
- ☐ Oregano
- ☐ Thyme
- ☐ Cinnamon
- ☐ Cloves
- ☐ Cardamom
- ☐ Dry Mint
- ☐ Saffron (store in the freezer section to retain its freshness)
- ☐ Ground cardamom (store in freezer section to retain its freshness)
- ☐ Ground coriander powder
- ☐ Ground cumin powder
- ☐ Sumac (a deep red powder found in Middle-Eastern grocery stores)
- ☐ Bay leaves
- ☐ Zahtar (a mixture of sesame seeds,ground sumac and thyme (see page :63)
- ☐ Garam Masala (East-Indian mixture of spices)

Hors d'oeuvres

Canadian Baked Samosas (Can Sams)
Makes : 12

These crowd pleasing low-fat Samosas will have your guests begging for more. They freeze well and can be reheated at 220°F until crisp. Delectable with the Decadent Date Chutney (page 37).

For the dough

2 cups unbleached white flour
1 tsp. baking soda
¾ tsp. salt, or to taste
¼ tsp. chili powder, or to taste
¾ cup nonfat yogurt or buttermilk
extra flour for kneading dough, as needed

- In a large bowl, combine all the ingredients to make a smooth dough, adding more flour as needed. Knead for 5 minutes.
- Refrigerate, covered, in an airtight container or in a plastic wrap, until you are ready to assemble the samosas.

For the filling:

2 tsp. canola oil
½ cup finely diced onion
1 tsp. cumin seeds
½ tsp. turmeric
½ tsp. chili powder, or to taste
1 tsp. brown sugar
1 tsp. garam masala (page 96) or Amti powder (page 114)
1 cup frozen green peas
½ cup finely diced green peppers
3 cups finely diced potatoes, **cooked until soft**
½ cup finely diced carrots, **steamed**
¾ tsp. salt, or to taste
¼ cup finely chopped coriander leaves

For the topping: Sesame seeds

Preparing the filling:

- Heat the oil in a large skillet over medium heat and sauté onions (with a pinch of salt) until golden brown. Add the cumin seeds, turmeric, chili powder, sugar and garam masala and sauté for 5 seconds.
- Add green peas and green pepper to the onion mixture. Stir. Cook, covered, for 5 minutes. Add the cooked potatoes, steamed carrots and the remaining ingredients. Stir thoroughly. Cook until heated right through, about 5 minutes. Remove the skillet from the heat and set aside to cool.

Assembling the Samosas :

- Preheat oven to 400°F.
- Divide the dough into 12 equal portions and roll into balls. Take one ball of dough. Roll it out very gently with a rolling pin to form thin rounds, about 8-inches in diameter. Place one heaping tablespoon of the vegetable filling in the centre of the rolled out dough.
- Form triangular pockets **to completely envelop the filling** by pulling two sides of the rolled dough together and joining with the third side. Brush the prepared samosa with a little water and cover the top with toasted sesame seeds. Transfer prepared samosa to a lightly greased baking sheet. Repeat procedure for remaining samosas.
- Using the lower rack of your oven, bake the samosas for 15 minutes. Reduce heat to 350°F and bake for another 10 minutes. (**For maximum crispness, turn the samosas over when you are turn the heat down**). Serve hot with dip of your choice.

Analysis per Samosa :
Calories (Kcal) : 123.4
Carbohydrate (g) : 23.4
Dietary Fiber (g) : 1.2
Protein (g) : 4.3
Sodium (mg) : 425

Total Fat (g) / % : 1.4 / 10.3 %
Saturated Fat (g) : 0.2
Monounsaturated Fat (g) : 0.6
Polyunsaturated Fat (g) : 0.5
Cholesterol (mg) : 0

Cheddar Bubble and Squeak   Serves : 6

You and your kids will squeal with delight when you taste these humongous squeaks that look like huge patties. Served with a salad, they make a light meal. They are simple and easy-to-prepare. I make smaller sized ones when I serve them as part of a larger meal.

4 medium potatoes, **cooked and lightly broken up**
2 cups diced cabbage, **steamed**
1 cup minced mushrooms
4 tbs. chopped, fresh parsley
4 egg whites, beaten lightly
¾ cup low-fat grated cheddar cheese
½ tsp. freshly ground nutmeg
salt and ground black pepper, to taste
rolled oats or oatbran , for coating patties
very little canola oil, for frying patties on both sides (about 1 tbs.)

- In a large bowl, add all the ingredients and knead till well incorporated. Divide and shape into 12 large patties. Chill for an hour before cooking.
- Dust both sides of the patties with a light coating of rolled oats.
- Heat a large nonstick skillet on medium-high heat. Lightly coat it with oil. Transfer patties to the skillet without overcrowding them and cook both sides until golden brown, about 4 minutes on each side. Drain on a paper towel. Serve hot and crisp.

Analysis per patty :
Calories (Kcal) : 110.5
Carbohydrate (g) : 11.3
Dietary Fiber (g) : 0.9
Protein (g) : 7.3
Sodium (mg) : 131

Total Fat (g) / % : 2.6 / 24.1 %
Saturated Fat (g) : 0.9
Monounsaturated Fat (g) : 1.4
Polyunsaturated Fat (g) : 0.2
Cholesterol (mg) : 3

Hockey Puck Latkes   Makes : 12

With these latkes you will score big with friends and family. The name for this recipe was coined by my husband because of their resemblance to hockey pucks. At your next Stanley Cup party instead of reaching for a handful of potato chips reach for a latke. These latkes are so good that even Don Cherry would give them the thumbs up! If made ahead, crisp them before serving, in a preheated oven at 200°F for 15 to 20 minutes.

4 medium potatoes, peeled, finely grated and set aside to drain
½ cup finely diced onions
2 tbs. chopped parsley or 1 tbs. dried parsley
5 egg-whites, well beaten + ½ cup water
¾ tsp. salt, or to taste
½ tsp. ground black pepper, or to taste
1 cup matzo meal **or** oatmeal
1 tsp. baking powder
1 tbs. canola oil for coating 12 cup muffin pan

- Preheat oven to 350°F. Lightly grease a muffin pan.
- Squeeze out any liquid left behind in the grated potatoes.
- In a large bowl, combine the well beaten eggs together with the remaining ingredients. Stir thoroughly until well combined.
- Fill the greased muffin pans half full. Bake for 15 minutes. At this point take the muffin pan out of the oven and flip the Latkes over and bake for another 15 minutes (check to see that both sides of the Latkes are golden brown).
- Remove from oven and serve hot with sour cream or apple sauce.

Analysis per latke :
Calories (Kcal) : 66.4
Carbohydrate (g) : 10.4
Dietary Fiber (g) : 1.2
Protein (g) : 3.1
Sodium (mg) : 101

Total Fat (g) / % : 1.5 / 20 %
Saturated Fat (g) : 0.2
Monounsaturated Fat (g) : 0.8
Polyunsaturated Fat (g) : 0.1
Cholesterol (mg) : 0

Note : Microwave Method to cook potatoes for the Double Baked Potatoes recipe on Page 24 :

Pierce the scrubbed potatoes all over with a fork. Sprinkle the potatoes with a little water, and cook on High Power (check your microwave oven book for cooking time & instructions) for 10 -12 minutes or until soft to the touch. Then, follow the "Double baked potato" recipe on page 24.

HOCKEY PUCK LATKES

Oven Baked Potato Wedges   Serves : 6

A satisfying alternative to oil drenched cottage fries. But beware. I find that if I am not strategic in serving them, there are usually none left by the time I get to the table. Partially cooking the potatoes beforehand saves baking time.

6 large baking potatoes with skins, scrubbed clean,halved lengthwise,
cut into wedges
½ tsp. salt or onion salt

Coating Ingredients:
2 tbs. cornstarch
1 tbs. canola oil
1 tsp. **each** paprika, ground allspice and grated parmesan cheese
salt, to taste

- Preheat the oven to 400°F.
- Transfer the cut potato wedges and salt to a pot of cold water and cook on high heat. When the water reaches a rolling boil, remove the potato wedges which are only partially cooked at this stage to a large bowl. Add the coating ingredients. Toss gently to coat all over.
- Lightly grease a baking sheet. Stand the coated potato wedges, skin side down on the baking sheet in a single layer, leaving space between each wedge.
- Bake for 20 minutes or until the potato wedges are cooked.
- Broil the baked wedges for 5 minutes or until they turn a beautiful golden brown all over. Serve immediately with the dip of your choice.

Analysis per serving:	
Calories (Kcal) : 122.9	Total Fat (g) / % : 2.6 /18.9 %
Carbohydrate (g) : 22.7	Saturated Fat (g) : 0.4
Dietary Fiber (g) : 1.8	Monounsaturated Fat (g) : 1.4
Protein (g) : 2.7	Polyunsaturated Fat (g) : 0.7
Sodium (mg) : 23	Cholesterol (mg) : 1

Double Baked Potatoes   Serves : 2

These are my husband's favorite snack/meal and have become a winner among friends and family. You can stretch your imagination and put your creative skills to work by coming up with your family's favorite fillings. Following the recipe are a few more ideas to start with. I hope you enjoy them as much as Chuck and I do.

2 Large Baking Potatoes, scrubbed clean, (cooking instructions on Page:22)

Egg Salad filling:
2 hard boiled egg-whites, chopped
2 tbs. finely chopped celery
3 tbs. finely chopped green onions
1 tbs. freshly chopped dill weed or 1 tsp. dry dill weed
1 tsp. Dijon mustard
2 tbs. nonfat yogurt
salt and ground black pepper, to taste

Topping: 2 tbs. low-fat cheddar cheese

Baking the Potatoes :
- Scrub the baking potatoes until clean. Pierce them all over with a fork and wrap individually in aluminum foil. Bake at 450^0F for an hour or until done. (microwave method on page: 22).
- Remove from the oven and when cool to the touch, cut in half lengthwise. Scoop out the cooked potato flesh, leaving the skins intact. Set aside the potato skins on a baking sheet.

Filling the Potato Skins:
- Combine the "egg salad filling" ingredients with the scooped out potato flesh. Mix thoroughly until well combined.
- Divide the filling evenly among the 4 prepared potato skins. Top each one with ½ tablespoon of the grated cheddar cheese.
- Put skins back on the baking sheet and bake a second time under the broiler for 6 to 8 minutes or until golden brown. Serve hot with Cheese and Chives Dip. (see page 38)

Analysis per serving : (with cheese)

Calories (Kcal) : 147.3 (167.2)	Total Fat (g) / % : 2.8/ 16.8 % (4/ 21.3%)
Carbohydrate (g) : 22.6 (22.8)	Saturated Fat (g) : 0.8 (1.6)
Dietary Fiber (g) : 2.1 (2.1)	Monounsaturated Fat (g) : 1 (1.4)
Protein (g) : 8.3 (10.3)	Polyunsaturated Fat (g) : 0.4 (0.5)
Sodium (mg) : 167 (204)	Cholesterol (mg) : 107(110)

Variation : Different Fillings

Cheese & Chives filling
1/2 cup finely chopped chives or green onions
2 tbs. no-fat mayonnaise or nonfat yogurt
1/4 cup finely chopped green pepper
1/2 cup chopped tomatoes, firm ones
2 tbs. grated parmesan cheese
salt and pepper, to taste
Topping: 2 tbs. grated low-fat mozzarella cheese

Mexican filling
2 tbs. finely chopped tomatoes
1/2 cup finely chopped red pepper
1/4 cup cooked red beans, mashed
2 tbs. fresh lime juice or lemon juice, or to taste
2 tbs. canned jalapeño peppers, finely chopped
Mexican chili powder, salt and pepper, to taste
Topping : 2 tbs. grated low-fat cheddar cheese

Masala filling
4 tbs. finely chopped red onions
1/4 cup finely chopped tomatoes
1 tsp. freshly grated ginger
1 green chili, seeded and finely chopped
1/2 tsp. garam masala (page 97)
2 tbs. each fresh lemon juice and finely chopped coriander leaves
salt and pepper, to taste

Cheese & Carrot Rolls   Makes : 18 pieces

These easy-to-prepare rolls can be assembled ahead of time and grilled when needed. I always made these for my daughter's birthday parties as the kids adored them. The rolls disappeared faster than lightning, especially when the kids competed to see who could outdo the other in eating .

6 slices fresh, whole wheat bread, crust removed

Filling Ingredients:
1 cup finely grated carrots
½ cup grated, low-fat mozzarella cheese **or** low-fat cheddar cheese
½ tsp. ground thyme
1 tsp. mustard powder
3 tbs. finely chopped green onions
lemon juice, salt and ground black pepper, to taste
Before baking - vegetable cooking spray to spray over the prepared rolls

- Using a rolling pin, flatten each bread slice until thin. Keep the rolled out slices covered with a wet cloth or napkin.
- Combine the "filling ingredients" in a medium sized bowl and divide the filling into 6 equal portions.
- Spread or place one portion of the filling on one end of the rolled out bread slice. Roll up tightly and secure with a couple of toothpicks. Cutting at an angle, divide each roll into 3 segments. Arrange on a greased baking sheet and spray them lightly with cooking spray. Repeat procedure for the remaining rolled bread and filling.
- Place the prepared rolls under a broiler for 5-6 minutes or until golden brown. They brown quickly, so keep a watchful eye.
- Serve hot with chutney or chili sauce.

Analysis per serving (one serving = 3 pieces) :	
Calories (Kcal) : 100.8	Total Fat (g) / % : 2.7 / 23.8 %
Carbohydrate (g) : 14.3	Saturated Fat (g) : 1.3
Dietary Fiber (g) : 1.8	Monounsaturated Fat (g) : 0.9
Protein (g) : 5.2	Polyunsaturated Fat (g) : 0.3
Sodium (mg) : 195	Cholesterol (mg) : 5

Half Moon Broccoli Quesidilla   Serves: 6

Try these crisp vegetable filled tortillas as a snack or a meal. This quick, no fuss, no mess recipe is sure to delight even the most finicky taste buds. This recipe will make broccoli lovers out of your children - an often difficult task. Alternatively, use your children's favourite filling in the tortilla, as an added incentive for them to eat.

6 large flour tortillas

Filling ingredients :
3 cups broccoli florets [small size florets] + 4 tbs. water
2 cups finely sliced mushrooms
½ cup finely chopped green onions
1 tsp. crushed garlic
¼ tsp. salt , or to taste
¼ tsp. **each** ground cumin, thyme, **and** chili powder, or to taste
1 cup grated, low-fat mozzarella cheese

- Steam broccoli sprayed with 4 tbs. of water, until fairly soft, for 6-8 minutes. Set aside to drain. When cool, combine with the filling ingredients.
- Heat a large nonstick skillet over medium-high heat. Take a tortilla and place it on a plate. Spread 1/6 of the broccoli mixture on one half of the tortilla. Fold the other half over, forming a half moon to cover the filling. Transfer it to the skillet. Apply light pressure on the folded tortilla with a spatula to speed up the cooking process.
- Cook the prepared tortilla until golden on both sides. Prepare the remaining tortillas in the same way. Serve them hot, topped with Tropical Salsa Cruda or dip of your choice.

Analysis per Quesidilla:
Calories (Kcal) : 198.3   Total Fat (g) / % : 6.1 / 27 %
Carbohydrate (g) : 26   Saturated Fat (g) : 2.5
Dietary Fiber (g) : 3.9   Monounsaturated Fat (g) : 2
Protein (g) : 11.2   Polyunsaturated Fat (g) : 1.3
Sodium (mg) : 331   Cholesterol (mg) : 10

Masala Vadas   Makes : 25 Pieces

These bite sized mini lentil patties disappear faster than the time it takes to prepare them. When we were kids, in India, this was a constant for our tiffin time (3 p.m. snack). We used to make tons of vadas and have them with masala tea. Those warm family memories give me a special feeling every time I make this recipe.

For grinding : (soak for 4 hours and drain before grinding)
2 cups split chick peas **+** ¼ cup raw rice
1 tsp. fennel seeds
2 tsp. finely diced ginger
2 dry red chili peppers

Add before frying : ½ cup **each** finely diced onion **and** coriander leaves
                               ½ tsp. salt, or to taste

Canola oil for deep frying :
Use 1 ¼ cups of oil for deep frying **(after frying , you will find that
                                less than 1/4 cup of oil was used)**

- Pulverize the **drained** "for grinding" ingredients, in a food processor or blender (adding very little water if needed), to a coarse consistency, like crushed nuts.. Transfer to a large bowl. Add diced onions, salt and coriander leaves to the ground mixture and mix well.
- Heat oil in a deep saucepan. When oil is hot enough **(test if ready by dropping in a piece of the ground mixture. If hot enough, it should rise up at once)**, make a walnut sized ball with the ground mixture. Flatten it in the palm of your hand and gently slide it into the hot oil. Put in as many vadas as your saucepan can accommodate and fry the vadas until golden brown.
- Remove and drain the fried vadas on absorbent paper towel.
- Serve hot with Decadent Date Chutney or dip of your choice.

Analysis per piece (per vada):

Calories (Kcal) : 84.9	Total Fat (g) / % : 1.3 / 32.8 %
Carbohydrate (g) : 11.3	Saturated Fat (g) : 0.3
Dietary Fiber (g) : 2.8	Monounsaturated Fat (g) : 1.5
Protein (g) : 3.3	Polyunsaturated Fat (g) : 1.1
Sodium (mg) : 80	Cholesterol (mg) : 0

Baked Falafel   Makes : 20 Falafels

This recipe is for the falafel fans who had requested of me a low-fat version of their favourite dish. This is a move away from the original deep fried version, but the taste remains intact. When I do serve falafel, this is what my family (especially the Rosens) and friends enjoy.

1 cup raw chick peas, **soaked overnight and drained**
2 slices whole-wheat bread, torn to bits
2 cloves garlic, minced
4 green onions, finely chopped
¼ cup minced coriander leaves **or** ¼ cup minced parsley
salt and ground black pepper, to taste
1 tsp. baking powder
½ tsp. baking soda
1 tsp. ground coriander
1 tsp. ground cumin
¼ tsp. crushed red pepper, or to taste

Make these accompaniments a day ahead (to release flavor)
   Homemade relish (page 41) and **Taratour sauce** (page 42)

- Preheat the oven to 350°F.
- Pulverize the chick peas in a food processor to a coarse consistency. Add the whole-wheat bread, garlic, green onions, coriander leaves, and parsley and whirl it until all the ingredients blend together and have the appearance of crushed nuts. Transfer the ground mixture to a medium-sized bowl and add the baking powder, baking soda, ground coriander, ground cumin and red pepper. Stir until well combined.
- Knead the ground ingredients and shape them into walnut sized balls. Flatten them slightly between your palms and place them on a non-stick baking sheet. Once you have shaped them all , bake them in a preheated oven for 8-10 minutes, ensuring not to overbake or make them too brown. Serve hot.
- Combine the relish ingredients. Refrigerate
- Combine the taratour sauce ingredients. Blend them together in a food processor or blender. Refrigerate.
- Serve falafels as an appetizer or inside a pita with homemade relish, taratour sauce and hot sauce.

Analysis per falafel :

Calories (Kcal): 47.8	Total Fat (g) / % : 0.5 / 8.4 %
Carbohydrate (g) : 9.2	Saturated Fat (g) : 0.1
Dietary Fiber (g) : 1.9	Monounsaturated Fat (g) : 0.1
Protein (g) : 2	Polyunsaturated Fat (g) : 0.2
Sodium (mg) :119	Cholesterol (mg) : 0

Variation: Serving suggestions:

As an appetizer :

- Serve on a bed of lettuce, using the taratour sauce for dipping.

Pita Sandwich :

- Heat the pita for a few seconds in the microwave oven or regular oven (makes it easy to open them).
- Cut the pita in half and open to make a pocket.
- Stuff the pita pockets with 3 falafels, a dollop of the homemade relish, some alfalfa sprouts, taratour sauce and hot sauce, to taste .

Frozen falafels :

- Baked falafels can be frozen and used instead of meatballs in spaghetti sauce.

In East-Indian curries :

- When I am low on vegetables, I use this as a filler. Not only do I have a protein filled dish, I have a curry with a twist.

Crunchy Bulgur Burgers   Serves : 6

A delight to the taste buds and visually pleasing. If necessity is the mother of invention, these bulgur patties are the invention of desperation. Each year I create a new recipe for our wedding anniversary. This year I had to come up with something delicious and nutritious, yet easy to prepare. So here it is. I serve these patties with pickled dill and steamed broccoli.

½ cup bulgur soaked in ½ cup warm water for ½ hour
1 cup cooked chick peas, **rinsed, drained and mashed**
2 medium potatoes, **cooked and lightly broken up**
3 tbs. whole wheat flour
¼ cup **each** chopped parsley **and** finely chopped green onion
1 tbs. crushed garlic
3 tbs. lemon juice, or to taste
2 tsp. **each** coriander powder **and** cumin powder, or to taste
½ tsp. **each** paprika **and** cinnamon
salt and ground black pepper, to taste
oatmeal for dusting the patties
1 tbs. canola oil, or, vegetable cooking spray for cooking patties

- In a large bowl, **except for the oatmeal**, combine all the ingredients to form a thick mixture. Divide the mixture into 6 equal portions. Shape them into large patties, 4-inches round and ¾-inch thick. Give them a good coating of the oatmeal and set aside.
- Cook the patties in a large nonstick skillet, sprayed with a little cooking spray on medium-high heat. Cook both sides until golden brown, spraying a little cooking spray, if needed.
- Serve patties with a light salad and some steamed vegetables.

Analysis per patty :	
Calories (Kcal) : 155.1	Total Fat (g) / % : 3.2 % 17.3
Carbohydrate (g) : 28.8	Saturated Fat (g) : 0.3
Dietary Fiber (g) : 5.3	Monounsaturated Fat (g) : 1.5
Protein (g) : 5.1	Polyunsaturated Fat (g) : 1
Sodium (mg) : 124	Cholesterol (mg) : 0

Pearl's Vegetarian Kishka   Serves: 6

Having a vegetarian daughter-in-law encouraged my mother-in-law, Pearl, to prepare this vegetarian version of a kishka. The combination of matzo meal and vegetables gives this recipe a unique, aromatic taste. It makes an excellent appetizer and goes well with any dip. Baked kishka can be frozen.

3 large carrots, finely grated
3 celery sticks, finely grated or minced
2 small potatoes, finely grated with skin
2 onions, finely grated
salt and ground black pepper, to taste
1 tbs. canola oil
2 ½ - 3 cups matzo meal or rolled oats

- Preheat the oven to 350°F.
- In a large bowl, combine all the ingredients. Mix thoroughly until well combined. Adjust seasoning to taste.
- Divide the mixture into 6 equal portions. Roll each portion into an 8-inch log and wrap it with aluminum foil. Place them on a baking sheet.
- Prepare the remaining kishka in a similar manner.
- Bake for 30 minutes. Serve hot with dip of your choice.

```
Analysis per Kishka :
Calories (Kcal) : 227.1          Total Fat (g) / % : 4.9 / 19.1 %
Carbohydrate (g) : 39            Saturated Fat (g) : 0.2
Dietary Fiber (g) : 7.1          Monounsaturated Fat (g) : 1.4
Protein (g) : 8                  Polyunsaturated Fat (g) : 0.8
Sodium (mg) : 624                Cholesterol (mg) : 0
```

Dips

Sauces

&

Chutneys

Cranberry Fruit Chutney   Makes:8 cups

Nutritionally, this chutney is far superior to the store bought version. I call it my 'palate teaser', and use it as a dip or in the place of a relish. I sometimes mix 1/2 cup of this luscious chutney with 1/2 cup nonfat yogurt or sour cream for a variation.

3 cups fresh cranberries, cleaned and set aside to drain
2 large tart apples, finely chopped
1 cup yellow raisins
1 whole orange, **seeded and chopped fine with skin**
1 tsp. freshly grated lemon rind
½ cup dark brown sugar
½ cup unsweetened orange juice concentrate **and** lemon juice
½ cup fresh lemon juice
½ cup apple cider vinegar
2 tbs. mustard seeds
¼ cup chopped crystallized ginger
1 tsp. **each** grated, fresh ginger root **and** minced jalapeño peppers
1 tsp. **each** ground cinnamon **and** ground cloves, or to taste
¼ tsp. dried hot pepper flakes
½ tsp. salt or to taste

- Combine all the ingredients in a large saucepan and cook over medium-high heat , without boiling, until sugar is dissolved.
- Bring to a boil. Simmer, uncovered, stirring occasionally, for about 1 hour or until the mixture is thick.
- Pour into hot sterilized jars, seal and refrigerate.

Analysis per serving (per tablespoon) :

Calories (Kcal) : 3.7	Total Fat (g) / % : 0/ 2.3%
Carbohydrate (g) : 0.9	Saturated Fat (.g) : 0
Dietary Fiber (g) : 0.1	Monounsaturated Fat (g) : 0
Protein (g) : 0.1	Polyunsaturated Fat (g) : 0
Sodium (mg) : 7	Cholesterol (mg) : 0

Hummus (Chick Pea Dip)   Serves : 6

This low-fat dip is a versatile filling for regular sandwiches and pita. To give it a wicked kick, try my spicy variation by adding 2 tablespoon canned jalapeñoes to the recipe. My husband, Chuck, revels in dipping fresh pita into Hummus. This is the traditional Middle-Eastern way of enjoying this dip.

For Grinding:
2 cups **cooked or canned** chick peas, **rinsed and drained**
2 tbs. toasted sesame seeds or 2 tbs. home-made tahini* *
2-3 small cloves of garlic
¼ cup lemon juice, or to taste
½ tsp. **each** salt **and** crushed black pepper, or to taste
1 tsp. cumin powder, or to taste
2 tbs. flat Italian parsley

Garnish : 2 tbs. fresh curly parsley, sliced tomatoes

- Grind together all the ingredients in a blender or food processor, adding a little water, if required.
- Serve garnished with a sprig of parsley, surrounded by sliced jicama (a root vegetable), celery sticks, carrot sticks and toasted pita.

Analysis per serving :

Calories (Kcal) : 117.6	Total Fat (g) / % : 2.6/ 19.5%
Carbohydrate (g) : 19.6	Saturated Fat (g) : 0.3
Dietary Fiber (g) : 3.6	Monounsaturated Fat (g) : 0.9
Protein (g) : 4.9	Polyunsaturated Fat (g) : 1,2
Sodium (mg) : 241	Cholesterol (mg) : 0

---

*Note: ** To make home-made tahini using a blender Grind on very high speed - 1 cup toasted sesame seeds with 1 tbs. water, to make a fine paste. Transfer to an airtight bottle / container and keep inverted to prevent lumping. Keeps well for a few months. Needs no refrigeration*

Tropical Salsa Cruda   Makes: 5 cups

A big batch disappears fast, when hungry folk are around. I use this as a dip, a side dish for a vegetable loaf or inside an omelet with a little cheese. There is no end to the way you can serve this easy-to-make dip.

2 cups freshly diced ripe tomatoes
½ cup tomato paste
2 cups canned crushed pineapple
2 cups diced mangoes
½ cup finely diced red onions
3 - 4 tbs. lime or lemon juice
½ cup finely chopped coriander leaves
1 tsp. **each** coriander powder **and** cumin powder, or to taste
2 - 3 tbs. finely chopped canned jalapeño peppers (page 90)
½ tsp. chili powder, or to taste
2 - 3 tbs. brown sugar
salt, to taste

- Soak diced onions in ice-cold water with a pinch of salt and a pinch of sugar for an hour (takes out the pungency of the onion, and makes it crisp). Set aside to drain, then refrigerate
- Mix the prepared onions with the remaining ingredients. Mash very lightly with back of spoon. Transfer to an air-tight container and refrigerate until ready to use.
- Makes an excellent dip or a side dish with vegetable burgers or steamed rice.

```
Analysis per serving ( 1/3 cup ) :
Calories (Kcal) : 38               Total Fat (g) / % : 0.3 / 5.9 %
Carbohydrate (g) : 940.9           Saturated Fat (g) : 0
Dietary Fiber (g) : 1.2            Monounsaturated Fat (g) : 0.1
Protein (g) : 0.7                  Polyunsaturated Fat (g) : 0.1
Sodium (mg) : 8                    Cholesterol (mg) : 0
```

Decadent Date Chutney   Makes: 2 cups

This exquisite tasting sweet chutney has a deep rich color. My friends always put this chutney on their wish list everytime I make Samosas although it goes well with any finger food. It can be stored for a few weeks, in the refrigerator, in an airtight container.

1 cup pitted dates, diced
1 cup raisins
2 cups hot water
3 tbs. brown sugar
2 tbs. tamarind paste or ¼ cup fresh lime juice
1 tsp. chili powder, or to taste
1 tbs. cumin powder, dry roasted in a skillet, over stove top
¾ tsp. salt, or to taste

- In a deep nonstick skillet bring the pitted dates, raisins and water to a boil. Reduce heat and cook for 5 minutes. Remove pan from heat and set aside to cool.
- Transfer the cooled dates and raisins to the food processor or blender bowl. Add the remaining ingredients and pulverize them in a blender or food processor, until smooth. This chutney maintains its fresh taste for a good two weeks. Refrigerate, covered, in an airtight container.
- Goes beautifully with Samosas and other appetizers like cheese and carrot rolls, spring rolls etc.

Analysis per Serving (1 tablespoon) :
Calories (Kcal) : 33   Total Fat (g) / % : 0.1/ 1.5 %
Carbohydrate (g) : 8.7   Saturated Fat (g) : 0
Dietary Fiber (g) : 0.6   Monounsaturated Fat (g) : 0
Protein (g) : 0.3   Polyunsaturated Fat (g) : 0
Sodium (mg) : 52   Cholesterol (mg) : 0

Cheese and Chives Dip   Makes: 2 cups

Harmonizes beautifully with double baked potatoes or crisp baked pita. You'll be singing its praises after your first mouthful of this savory condiment. It is smooth and delicious and should be made a few hours before serving to fully release its awesome flavors.

1 cup nonfat yogurt cheese (see below, for instructions)
1 cup nonfat sour cream
2 tbs. grated parmesan **or** grated romano cheese
6 tbs. finely chopped chives
salt and freshly ground black pepper, to taste

- Combine all the ingredients and serve well chilled.

Analysis per serving (per tablespoon) :

Calories (Kcal) : 13.4	Total Fat (g) / % : 0.1/ 8.8%
Carbohydrate (g) : 1.7	Saturated Fat (g) : 0.1
Dietary Fiber (g) : 0	Monounsaturated Fat (g) : 0
Protein (g) : 1.4	Polyunsaturated Fat (g) : 0
Sodium (mg) : 55	Cholesterol (mg) : 1

Note : ***Home-made Yogurt Cheese

To get 2 cups of yogurt cheese you will require 4 cups of nonfat yogurt.

♥ *Spoon yogurt into a sieve (lined with a cheese cloth or coffee filter) and place it over a deep bowl. Let it remain undisturbed in the refrigerator, overnight. Next day, use the yogurt cheese as desired.*

Some helpful hints on where you could use yogurt cheese:

♥ *I use the nutrient laden whey to make bread .*
♥ *If a recipe calls for cream cheese ,I substitute with yogurt cheese.*
♥ *Makes an excellent bagel topping .*
♥ *I use it for cheese topping on cakes.*
♥ *Use it in place of sour cream*

Velvety Vanilla Yogurt Dip   Makes: 2 cups

Excellent over toasted bagel, cakes, or even as a topping for a light carrot cake instead of the fat filled cream cheese topping. Great over fresh fruit salad. Believe me, it tastes as good as it sounds.

1 cup nonfat yogurt cheese (page 38 for recipe)
1 cup nonfat sour cream
1 tbs. vanilla extract
3 tbs. sugar or sweetener of your choice

- Combine and serve well chilled as a dip or as a cake topping.

Analysis per serving : (per tablespoon)
Calories (Kcal) : 15.3	Total Fat (g) / % : 0 / 2.4%
Carbohydrate (g) : 2.5	Saturated Fat (g) : 0
Dietary Fiber (g) : 0	Monounsaturated Fat (g) : 0
Protein (g) : 1.2	Polyunsaturated Fat (g) : 0
Sodium (mg) : 16	Cholesterol (mg) : 0

Fruit Raita   Makes: 3 cups

This lively fruit salad in yogurt augments any rice dish like Vegetable Biryani or Paella or can stand on its own as a light dessert.

2 cups non-fat yogurt + a pinch of salt
2 cups canned, mixed fruit cocktail, drained
2 tbs. sugar or sweetener of your choice

- Combine and serve well chilled.

Analysis per serving : (per tablespoon)
Calories (Kcal) : 15.3	Total Fat (g) / % : 0 / 2.4%
Carbohydrate (g) : 2.5	Saturated Fat (g) : 0
Dietary Fiber (g) : 0	Monounsaturated Fat (g) : 0
Protein (g) : 1.2	Polyunsaturated Fat (g) : 0
Sodium (mg) : 16	Cholesterol (mg) : 0

Herbed Bean Paté　　　　Makes : 3 cups

The baby pink color combined with the fresh aroma of the roasted peppers makes this a deeply satisfying dip. Leftovers make good fillings in Mexican Lasagna or in Volcanic Enchiladas.

2 red peppers, cut in half and seeded
4 - 6 cloves garlic, with skin on
½ tsp. canola oil
1 small red onion, quartered
2 cups canned white beans, **rinsed clean and drained**
4 tbs. fresh thyme **or 2 tbs. dried** thyme
¼ cup fresh lemon juice, or to taste
¾ tsp. salt, or to taste

- Roast the red peppers and garlic under a broiler. When the outside of the red pepper and garlic have a charred appearance, remove them from the oven.
- When cool to the touch, remove the burnt skin from the red pepper. Set aside.
- Squeeze out the pulp from the baked garlic cloves. Set aside.
- Using a small frying pan, sauté the red onion until translucent.
- Transfer the sautéed onions, cooked beans, roasted pepper and garlic and the remaining ingredients to a food processor or blender and pulverize them to a fine consistency Adjust seasoning to taste.
- Transfer to a greased container and pack in the ground bean mixture. Refrigerate for a few hours, before serving.
- Just before serving, invert onto a serving platter and serve surrounded by fresh vegetables.
- Goes well with crisp pita wedges or bagel chips or as a filling in a pita sandwich and even as a dip with freshly cut carrots and celery.

Analysis per serving (per tablespoon) :	
Calories (Kcal) : 16.2	Total Fat (g) / % : 0.1 / 5.3%
Carbohydrate (g) : 3.1	Saturated Fat (g) : 0
Dietary Fiber (g) : 0.7	Monounsaturated Fat (g) : 0
Protein (g) : 0.9	Polyunsaturated Fat (g) : 0
Sodium (mg) : 34	Cholesterol (mg) : 0

Homemade Relish   Makes : 2 cups

An alternative to store bought relish in its appearance and taste. I use it as a filling for my pita pockets; especially for falafel sandwiches.

2 cups diced tomatoes + 3 tbs. fresh lemon juice
1/2 cup **each** minced cucumber **and** minced green pepper
1 tbs. **each** minced parsley **and** minced cilantro
salt **and** hot chili sauce, **to taste**

- Combine all the ingredients in a medium-sized bowl and serve well chilled

Analysis per serving (per tablespoon) :	
Calories (Kcal) : 3.1	Total Fat (g) / % : 0 / 9.9%
Carbohydrate (g) : 0.7	Saturated Fat (g) : 0
Dietary Fiber (g) : 0.2	Monounsaturated Fat (g) : 0
Protein (g) : 0.1	Polyunsaturated Fat (g) : 0
Sodium (mg) : 1	Cholesterol (mg) : 0

✳✳✳✳✳✳✳✳✳✳✳✳✳✳

Verdant Pesto   Makes : 2 cups

This non-traditional piquant pesto has the true flavor and texture of the original pesto, minus the olive oil. In the summer, my garden abounds with fresh basil which I use to make large batches of this pesto. Freezes well. Defrosted, it tastes as good as fresh pesto. Try this pesto over toasted bagel. It's heavenly!!

4 packed cups fresh basil, washed cleaned and set aside to drain
3 jalapeño peppers, seeded and chopped, or to taste
2 tbs. pine nuts, **dry toasted in a skillet for 5 minutes, on medium-high heat**
1/4 cup grated parmesan
3 - 4 tbs. flavored vinegar for grinding all of the above
salt, to taste

- Using a blender, grind to a fine consistency all the pesto ingredients.
- Store refrigerated in an airtight container. (This pesto can be frozen in airtight containers) .

Analysis per serving (per tablespoon) :	
Calories (Kcal) : 23.2	Total Fat (g) / % : 1.2/ 40.2 %
Carbohydrate (g) : 2.3	Saturated Fat (g) : 0.3
Dietary Fiber (g) : 0.2	Monounsaturated Fat (g) : 0.4
Protein (g) : 1.7	Polyunsaturated Fat (g) : 0.4
Sodium (mg) : 25	Cholesterol (mg) : 1

✳✳✳✳✳✳✳✳✳✳✳✳✳✳

Taratour Sauce
Makes : 1 cup

A low-fat sauce ideal for falafels or as a dip for vegetables. Goes well over steamed vegetables.

2 tbs. homemade tahini (page 35)
½ cup **each** lemon juice and nonfat yogurt
1 tsp. sugar or sweetener of your choice
¼ cup water
1 tbs. crushed garlic

• Blend all of the above ingredients to a fine consistency and refrigerate.

Analysis per serving (per tablespoon) :

Calories (Kcal) : 18.6	Total Fat (g) / % : 1 / 45.8%
Carbohydrate (g) : 1.9	Saturated Fat (g) : 0.2
Dietary Fiber (g) : 0.2	Monounsaturated Fat (g) : 0.4
Protein (g) : 0.8	Polyunsaturated Fat (g) : 0.5
Sodium (mg) : 6	Cholesterol (mg) : 0

✳✳✳✳✳✳✳✳✳✳✳✳✳✳

Tzaziki
Makes: 3 cups

This versatile Greek recipe can be called a dip, a side dish or even a salad. It blends well with any food and is handy to have in your refrigerator, especially on hot days when the mouth craves for something cooling.

1 cup nonfat yogurt cheese (page 38)
2 cups nonfat sour cream, drained of all water
1 small cucumber, seeded, grated and set aside to drain
2 small cloves garlic, crushed fine

• Combine all the ingredients in a medium bowl and serve well chilled.

Analysis per serving (per tablespoon) :

Calories (Kcal) : 11.6	Total Fat (g) / % : 0.1/ 3.9%
Carbohydrate (g) : 1.7	Saturated Fat (g) : 0
Dietary Fiber (g) : 0.1	Monounsaturated Fat (g) : 0
Protein (g) : 1.1	Polyunsaturated Fat (g) : 0
Sodium (mg) : 15	Cholesterol (mg) : 0

✳✳✳✳✳✳✳✳✳✳✳✳✳✳

Hearty

Soups

Cajun Corn Soup   Serves : 6

This nutrition-packed soup accents any cuisine or can be served with corn muffins or bread rolls. Smooth and filling, the corn kernels and swiss chard complement each other beautifully.

1 tsp. canola oil
1 cup finely diced onions
1 tbs. crushed garlic
4 bay leaves
1 tbs. Italian seasoning
¼ tsp. **each** crushed red pepper **and** ground black pepper, or to taste
1 cup finely chopped celery
3 cups diced tomatoes + 1 tbs. brown sugar
6 cups water
1 cup fresh corn kernels
1 cup shredded swiss chard **or** spinach
½ cup finely diced green or red pepper
¾ cup **cooked** black-eyed beans
½ tsp. salt, or to taste

- Heat the oil in a large soup pot or Dutch oven over medium-high heat and sauté onions (with a pinch of salt) until golden brown. Add the garlic and spices and sauté for 5 seconds.
- Add the celery, tomatoes, brown sugar and water and cook, covered on medium-high heat, for 15 minutes.
- Add the corn kernels, swiss chard or spinach, green peppers, cooked black-eyed beans. and salt. Stir well to combine. Adjust seasoning to taste. Cover and simmer for 5 to 8 minutes.
- Discard the bay leaves before serving the soup.
- Spoon into individual bowls and serve hot with bread of your choice,

Analysis per serving:
Calories (Kcal) : 169.9
Carbohydrate (g) : 33.6
Dietary Fiber (g) : 5.8
Protein (g) : 6.2
Sodium (mg) : 131

Total Fat (g) / % : 3.6 / 16.8 %
Saturated Fat (g) : 0.4
Monounsaturated Fat (g) : 1.6
Polyunsaturated Fat (g) : 1.3
Cholesterol (mg) : 0

Potato & Barley Soup   Serves : 6

Since I found cooking regular barley tedious, I experimented with barley flakes and the result was amazing. Besides saving time, this method makes the soup creamier and tastier. Since then, everytime I teach this recipe to my students, they are thrilled to learn of this shortcut method which is easier than using regular barley.

¾ cup barley flakes **+ 4 cups water to cook the barley flakes**
1 tsp. oil
½ cup finely chopped onion
1 tbs. crushed garlic
1 tbs. dry vegetable broth mix, or to taste (page 46)
4 bay leaves
4 medium potatoes, ½-inch cubes
1 cup **each** diced carrots **and** celery
2 cups water or more, if required
salt and ground black pepper, to taste

- In a large Dutch oven, combine barley flakes with 4 cups hot water and cook on medium-high heat for 10 minutes.
- Meanwhile, heat oil in a small nonstick skillet over medium-high heat and sauté onions (with a pinch of salt) until translucent, about 3 minutes. Add garlic, dry vegetable broth mix and bay leaves and sauté for 5 seconds. Transfer this mixture and the remaining ingredients to the barley that's cooking.
- Cook covered until both the barley and vegetables are soft, about 20 minutes. Adjust seasoning to taste. Discard bay leaves before serving. Spoon into individual bowls and serve hot, after 10 minutes.

Analysis per serving :	
Calories (Kcal) : 115.6	Total Fat (g) / % : 1.2/9.3 %
Carbohydrate (g) : 23.7	Saturated Fat (g) : 0.2
Dietary Fiber (g) : 4.5	Monounsaturated Fat (g) : 0.6
Protein (g) : 3.5	Polyunsaturated Fat (g) : 0.3
Sodium (mg) : 78	Cholesterol : 0

Dry Vegetable Broth Mix
(all ingredients used in this broth mix are dry)

This broth mix augments cream style soups. For added flavor, try adding a tablespoon of this broth mix when cooking rice or when baking vegetable loaves.

4 tbs. onion powder
4 tbs. onion flakes
4 tbs. garlic powder
4 tbs. parsley
4 tbs. chives
1 tbs. celery salt
1 tbs. marjoram
1 tbs. thyme
1 tbs. basil
1 tbs. oregano
1 tbs. crushed dry dill weed
1 tsp. crushed chili flakes, or to taste
1 tsp. freshly ground black pepper ,or to taste

♦ Combine and store in an airtight container.
♦ Stir well, before each use.

Cabbage & Potato Soup   Serves : 6

Cabbage lovers savor this light, satisfying soup that is easy on the stomach and certainly easy to put together. I teach this recipe when students ask for a cabbage soup or I make it for my husband. Not a big fan of cabbage, I fall back on my trusted Upma (see page: 95) while he indulges in this soup.

1 tsp. canola oil
1 cup finely diced onions
4 cups shredded cabbage
2 cups diced potatoes (with skin)
1 cup grated carrots
5 cups water
3 cups canned tomatoes in juice, broken up
5 cups fresh tomatoes, chopped
3 - 4 tbs. fresh lemon juice, or to taste
1 tbs. sugar or sweetener of your choice
¾ tsp. dried thyme
¾ tsp. crushed basil
salt and and freshly ground black pepper, to taste

- Heat oil in a large soup pot over medium-high heat and sauté onions (with a pinch of salt) until translucent, about 3 minutes.
- Add the remaining ingredients. Simmer and cook until vegetables are soft to the touch and well combined, about 45 minutes.
- Spoon into individual bowls. Serve hot with bread of your choice.

Analysis per serving :
Calories (Kcal) : 70.2   Total Fat (g) / % : 1.3/14.9 %
Carbohydrate (g) : 14.3   Saturated Fat (g) : 0.1
Dietary Fiber (g) : 2.6   Monounsaturated Fat (g) : 0.5
Protein (g) : 2.2   Polyunsaturated Fat (g) : 0.5
Sodium (mg) : 122   Cholesterol (mg) : 0

Potaje Murciano (Red Bean Soup)   Serves : 6

This simple yet filling soup is a good choice when you are thinking of a " quick meal ". A complete meal in itself, it makes a nutritious lunch.

2 cups **cooked or canned** red kidney beans, **rinsed and drained**
1 cup cooked rice
1 tsp. olive oil
1 cup finely diced onions
4 cloves crushed garlic
3 bay leaves
1 tsp. **each** ground cumin **and** oregano, or to taste
½ tsp. **each** cayenne pepper **and** ground black pepper, or to taste
2 cups fresh green beans, cut into 1-inch pieces
4 cups water or more if required
2 cups finely diced tomatoes
2 tsp. brown sugar
2 tbs. red wine vinegar
½ tsp. salt, or to taste

- Heat oil in a large soup pot or Dutch oven over medium-high heat and sauté onions (with a pinch of salt) until golden brown. Add garlic and the remaining spices and sauté for 5 seconds.
- Add the **fresh green beans** and 4 cups water. Cover and cook for 15 minutes or until green beans are cooked.
- Add the tomatoes, brown sugar and red wine vinegar and cook until tomatoes go soft.
- Add the cooked kidney beans, cooked rice and salt. Adjust seasoning to taste. Bring the whole soup to a rolling boil. Let stand for 10 minutes to allow spices release their flavor. This soup is thick.
- Spoon into individual bowls and serve with bread of your choice.

Analysis per serving :
Calories (Kcal) : 159.9
Carbohydrate (g) : 31.3
Dietary Fiber (g) : 8
Protein (g) : 7
Sodium (mg) : 665

Total Fat (g) / % : 1.5 / 7.9 %
Saturated Fat (g) : 0.2
Monounsaturated Fat (g) : 0.6
Polyunsaturated Fat (g) : 0.4
Cholesterol (mg) : 0

Tomato Rasam   Serves : 6

This East-Indian soup is light and delicious. It makes a good starter soup before a heavy meal. For an even lighter version, reduce cooked lentils to 2 tablespoons.

For grinding:
5 large, overripe Roma tomatoes
3 cloves garlic
4 cups water
½ cup **cooked** lentils (split mung beans- yellow color)
1/8 tsp. ground turmeric (optional)
2 tbs. coriander seeds, **dry toasted and powdered** * *
1 tbs. cumin seeds, **dry toasted and powdered** * *
¼ tsp. **each** salt **and** ground black pepper, or to taste
½ tsp. ground asafetida* **(see next page for information)**
2 tsp. brown sugar or sweetener of your choice

Garnish:
2 to 3 tbs. fresh lemon juice or more, if desired
1 ripe Roma tomato, diced fine
4 tbs. finely chopped coriander leaves
½ cup baked croutons (optional)

- In a blender, grind the "for grinding" ingredients to a fine consistency
- Transfer the ground tomato mixture to a large soup pot or Dutch oven and bring it to a boil on medium heat. Take it off the heat.
- **To serve :** Spoon into individual soup bowls.
- **Before serving :** Add fresh lemon juice to taste. Garnish with diced tomatoes, coriander leaves and a few baked croutons.

Analysis per serving : (with croutons)	
Calories (Kcal) : 63.2 (85.4)	Total Fat (g) / % : 0.5/6.5 % (0.8/ 7.9 %)
Carbohydrate (g) : 13 (17.2)	Saturated Fat (g) : 0.1 (0.1)
Dietary Fiber (g) : 3.9 (4.1)	Monounsaturated Fat (g) : 0.1 (0.2)
Protein (g) : 3.5 (4.1)	Polyunsaturated Fat (g) : 0.2 (0.3)
Sodium (mg) : 13 (58)	Cholesterol (mg) : (0)

Note : Important Information

* *Asafetida : This pungent spice, of East-Indian origin is found only in East-Indian grocery stores. It is a resinous gum that is available in its lumpy or ground form. Use in small portions. For ease, I use the ground form. This spice has numerous beneficial properties, the most important one being an aid to digestion and relieving flatulence. In India, most bean recipes have a pinch of asafetida added, for easy digestion*

** Dry toasting and preserving spices

Heat a deep skillet over medium heat for 2 minutes. Add the spice you need toasted and dry toast, stirring every few seconds, for 5 - 7 minutes or until the aroma of the spice is released. Remove from heat and let cool for a few minutes. Grind in a spice or coffee grinder until reduced to a fine powder. Cool and store in airtight container, in a cool , dark place. I, store my ground spices, especially Amti powder, Garam Masala, and Tandoori Masala, in airtight bottles, in the freezer section, to retain their freshness.

Homemade Tandoori Masala

3 tbs. each coriander seeds, cumin seeds & fenugreek seeds
4 whole cinnamon sticks, each 3-inches long
Seeds of 12 whole cardamoms
2 tbs. each cloves & black pepper
1 tbs. ground ginger
1/4 cup paprika, or to taste
1 tsp. cayenne pepper, or to taste
2 tbs. ground dried fenugreek leaves, optional

Please follow the preparation instructions as in "Dry toasting and preserving ground spices"(see above) .

Pasta E Fagioli (Pasta &Bean Soup)   Serves : 6

his recipe went through heavy modifications before I came up with this perfect version. It was certified authentic by my Italian friend's mother (who couldn't believe it was low-fat). The pasta I use for this soup is Orzo (a pasta that resembles rice).

1 tsp. olive oil
1 cup finely diced onions
1 tbs. crushed garlic
1 - 2 tbs. Italian seasoning
2 cups diced carrots
2 cups diced celery
2 cups canned, crushed tomatoes
1 tbs. brown sugar or sweetener of your choice
6 cups water
½ cup small uncooked pasta (such as orzo, buttini)

To be added last:
>2 cups **canned** romano or red kidney beans, **rinsed and drained**
>1 cup diced red or green pepper, diced
>salt and ground black pepper, to taste

Garnish:
>½ cup chopped parsley
>2 tbs. grated parmesan cheese (optional)

- Heat the oil in a soup pot or Dutch oven over medium-high heat and sauté onions (with a pinch of salt) until golden brown. Add garlic and the Italian seasoning and sauté for a 10 seconds.
- Add the carrots, celery, crushed tomatoes, brown sugar and the water. Cook covered, on medium heat, for 20 minutes. Add the pasta and continue cooking until both the pasta and the vegetables are soft, about 10 minutes.
- Add the cooked beans, red or green peppers, salt and pepper, adding more water if soup is too thick. Stir thoroughly and cook covered on medium heat for another 5 minutes, Add parsley. Serve after 10 minutes.
- Spoon into individual bowls. Serve with freshly grated parmesan cheese, if desired.

Analysis per serving : (with parmesan cheese)

Calories (Kcal) : 166.4 (174)   Total Fat (g) / % : 1.6/8.2 % (2.1 /10.3%)

Carbohydrate (g) : 32.2 (32.3)   Saturated Fat (g) : 0.2 (0.5)

Dietary Fiber (g) : 8.9 (8.9)   Monounsaturated Fat (g) : 0.6 (0.8)

Protein (g) : 7.7 (8.4)   Polyunsaturated Fat (g) : 0.4 (0.4.)

Sodium (mg) : 782 (813)   Cholesterol (mg) : 0 (1))

Manchurian Soup   Serves : 6

In Taiwan, the Buddhist restaurants serve this soup as part of their 3 course or any course meal. I fell in love with this palate teasing soup that floods you with warmth at the very first sip. You can experience the different levels of heat with each sip. This soup is a constant in our home, especially in winter. Goes well with a bowl of steamed rice.

1 tsp. canola oil
½ cup finely diced onions
2 tsp. finely grated ginger
2 tsp. crushed garlic
3 cups **finely diced mixed** vegetables : beans, cabbage, cauliflower,
                              carrot, green or red pepper and celery
½ cup finely chopped green onions
6 cups water

Spices to be mixed in a small bowl
    3 tbs. cornstarch + ½ cup warm water
    2 tbs. **each** rice vinegar **&** low sodium soya sauce, or to taste
    4 tbs. fresh lemon juice, or to taste
    2 tsp. brown sugar or sweetener of your choice
    1 tsp. sweet chili sauce, or to taste
    salt **and** ground black pepper, to taste

Garnish : 1 egg-white, well beaten for flower effect
        Freshly chopped coriander leaves to taste

- Heat the oil in a large soup pot or Dutch oven over medium-high heat and sauté onions (with a pinch of salt) until translucent, about 3 minutes. Add the ginger and garlic and sauté for a minute. Add the prepared vegetables, green onions and water. Bring to a boil. Lower heat to medium. Cook until vegetables are soft (about 20 minutes).
- Add the prepared cornstarch and spice mixture to the soup. Stir well to combine. Adjust seasoning to taste. Bring to a gentle boil.
- Add the beaten egg-whites, very gradually, into the boiling soup. Boil for a minute, stirring constantly. Remove from the heat.
- Spoon into individual bowls. Garnish with coriander leaves.

Analysis per serving :

Calories (Kcal) : 109.9

Carbohydrate (g) : 20.7

Dietary Fiber (g) : 5.5

Protein (g) : 5.5

Sodium (mg) : 330

Total Fat (g) / % : 1.1 / 8.9 %

Saturated Fat (g) : 0.1

Monounsaturated Fat (g) : 0.5

Polyunsaturated Fat (g) : 0.4

Cholesterol (mg) : 0

Vegetable Dal (Lentil Soup)   Serves : 6

This is a popular soup in East-Indian households and restaurants. Skip the skim milk step for an elegant side dish.

1 cup **raw** split peas, **cooked in 3 cups water until soft**
1 tsp. **each** butter **and** canola oil
½ cup finely chopped onion
½ tsp. turmeric
1 tsp. garam masala, or to taste (see page : 114)
½ cup **each** finely chopped carrot, celery **&** red pepper
2 large tomatoes, finely pureed
2 cups water
½ tsp. **each** salt **&** ground black pepper, or to taste
½ cup skim milk mixed in 1 tsp. cornstarch, no lumps

Garnish: Freshly chopped coriander, to taste

- Heat butter and oil in a deep nonstick Dutch oven over medium heat and sauté onions (with a pinch of salt) until golden brown. Add the turmeric and garam masala and stir for 5 seconds. Add the carrots, celery and red pepper. Sauté for 5 minutes.
- Add the puréed tomatoes, water and the **cooked split peas**. Cook covered on medium-high heat, until vegetables are soft, about 10 minutes. Adjust seasoning to taste.
- Incorporate the skim milk mixture, very gradually, using a whisk or hand held electric beater. The soup should have a smooth look to it.
- Cook **uncovered**, on low heat, to heat the soup thoroughly.
- Spoon into individual soup bowls and serve hot, garnished with chopped coriander leaves.

Analysis per serving :	
Calories (Kcal) : 120.1	Total Fat (g) / % : 2 / 14.5 %
Carbohydrate (g) : 19.9	Saturated Fat (g) : 0.6
Dietary Fiber (g) : 6.9	Monounsaturated Fat (g) : 0.8
Protein (g) : 6.9	Polyunsaturated Fat (g) : 0.5
Sodium (mg) : 80	Cholesterol (mg) : 2

Two key ingredients qualify this soup as exquisite - its exotic taste and exquisite looks. I love the addition of canned jalapeño peppers which gives it a truly remarkable twist.

1 tsp. canola oil
¼ cup finely diced onions
1 tsp. **each** finely grated ginger **&** crushed garlic
3 cups cream style corn **+** 3 cups hot water

Spices to be mixed in a small bowl

> 1 tbs. cornstarch + ¼ cup warm water
> 2 tbs. **each** rice vinegar **&** low sodium soya sauce, or to taste
> 2 tbs. fresh lemon juice, or to taste
> 2 tsp. sugar or sweetener of your choice
> salt and ground black pepper, to taste

Garnish : ¼ cup finely chopped green onions
> freshly chopped coriander leaves, to taste
> canned jalapeño peppers, to taste

- Heat the oil in a large soup pot or Dutch oven over medium-high heat and sauté onions (with a pinch of salt) until golden brown Add the ginger and garlic and sauté for a minute. Add the cream style corn and water and bring to a gentle, rolling boil, stirring occasionally.
- Lower heat to medium. Add the prepared cornstarch/spice mixture. Stir well to combine. Adjust seasoning to taste. When it comes to a gentle boil, remove from heat.
- Spoon into individual bowls. Garnish with green onions, a few chopped coriander leaves and canned jalapeño peppers.

Analysis per serving :

Calories (Kcal) : 64.9	Total Fat (g) / % : 1.0 / 12.6
Carbohydrate (g) : 14.5	Saturated Fat (g) : 0.1
Dietary Fiber (g) : 0.4	Monounsaturated Fat (g) : 0.5
Protein (g) : 1.3	Polyunsaturated Fat (g) : 0.3
Sodium (mg) : 304	Cholesterol (mg) : 0

Salads

&

Dressings

My carrappleslaw is formidable competition for traditional coleslaw. This colorful diversion is worth trying. For a variation, add ½ cup of finely julienned jicama (a root vegetable) sticks.

Salad ingredients:

2 cups coarsely grated carrot
2 cups finely julienned cabbage
2 cups finely julienned apples [**mixed with 1 tbs. lemon juice to prevent it from discoloring**]
½ cup finely chopped green onions
½ cup finely julienned red pepper
½ cup raisins

Garnish:

3 tbs. sunflower seeds [optional]
¼ cup finely chopped parsley

Suggested dressing: Coleslaw dressing [page 72]

- In a large salad bowl, combine the salad ingredients. Refrigerate.
- Drizzle dressing over the prepared salad. Toss well to combine.
- At the very end, add the sunflower seeds [this helps retain its crunchiness] and parsley.
- Arrange prepared salad on a bed of lettuce or serve as is.

Analysis per serving : (with sunflower seeds)

Calories (Kcal) : 84 (109.7)	Total Fat (g) / % : 0.3 / 3.2 % (2.6 / 19.1%)
Carbohydrate (g) : 21.2 (22)	Saturated Fat (g) : 0.1 (0.3)
Dietary Fiber (g) : 2.2 (3.4)	Monounsaturated Fat (g) : 0 (0.5)
Protein (g) : 1.3 (2.3)	Polyunsaturated Fat (g) : 0.1 (1.6)
Sodium (mg) : 68 (68)	Cholesterol (mg) : 0 (0)

The McBean Salad   Serves : 6

This is a salad to which Canadian rowers Marnie McBean and Kathleen Heddle would cheerfully award the Olympic gold. With the addition of each ingredient, it bursts forth with breathtaking color. This salad is a medley of colors, flavors, textures and aromas. The first time I made this on television, the host started salivating and said to me, "This is bad for my image ..... people seeing me drooling over a salad !"

Salad Ingredients:

1 cup **cooked** red beans, **rinsed and drained**
1 cup **cooked** black beans, **rinsed and drained**
2 cups **canned** corn, **rinsed and drained**
1 green apple, finely diced
2 cups finely chopped celery
½ cup finely diced red pepper
½ cup finely diced green pepper
½ cup finely chopped red onions
½ cup finely chopped green onions

Suggested Dressing : Mexican Dressing: (page 71)

To serve : 4 to 6 large tortillas, broiled for 5 minutes (Insert a tortilla in an 8-inch pie pan to give a hollow starfish-like shape), or until golden and crisp.

- In a large bowl combine the "salad ingredients".
- Drizzle dressing over the prepared salad. Stir well to combine.
- Serve salad well chilled in individually prepared tortilla shells.

Analysis per serving : (with tortilla shell)
Calories (Kcal) : 222 (335.8)   Total Fat (g) / % : 1.1 / 4.2 % (3.6 / 9.3 %)
Carbohydrate (g) : 44.1 (63.6)   Saturated Fat (g) : 0.2(0.6)
Dietary Fiber (g) : 12.9 (14)   Monounsaturated Fat (g) : 0.2 (1.2)
Protein (g) : 12.6 (15.7)   Polyunsaturated Fat (g) : 0.5 (1.5)
Sodium (mg) : 355 (522)   Cholesterol (mg) : 0 (0)

Rojak (Malaysian Salad)   Serves : 6

In Singapore, this vegetable and pineapple salad is a regular at the Malaysian hawker stalls. I love the freshness and sweetness of the pineapple. It is normally served as an accompaniment to a main meal.

Salad Ingredients

1 seedless cucumber, halved lengthwise and sliced ½-inch thick
1 cup fresh pineapple chunks, 1-inch cubes
1 red pepper, diced into 1-inch pieces
1 green pepper, diced into 1-inch pieces

Suggested Dressing : Malaysian Dressing (page 71)

Garnish:
1 cup bean sprouts, cleaned and drained dry
2 tomatoes, medium diced

- In a large bowl, combine the salad vegetables. Refrigerate.
- **Just before serving :** In a large salad bowl, combine the prepared "salad ingredients", the dressing, bean sprouts and tomatoes. Adjust dressing to taste.
- Toss well to combine and serve immediately.
- Alternatively, the dressing can be served separately.

```
Analysis per serving :
Calories (Kcal) : 39.7              Total Fat (g) / % : 0.4 % / 7.6 %
Carbohydrate (g) : 9.1              Saturated Fat (g) : 0.1
Dietary Fiber (g) : 2               Monounsaturated Fat (g) : 0
Protein (g) : 1.6                   Polyunsaturated Fat (g) : 0.2
Sodium (mg) : 6                     Cholesterol (mg) : 0
```

Andalusian Salad   Serves : 6

This salad, a prize winner in the "Summer Salad Festival - 1995" sponsored by the Heart and Stroke Foundation, has been a mega hit with every person who has tasted it. I have received rave reviews for this salad, and I hope when you make it, it will give you the same satisfaction.

Salad Ingredients:

2 cups finely chopped celery
1 cup finely diced green pepper
1 cup finely diced red pepper
½ cup finely chopped green onions
2 cups **cooked** rice, cold or at room temperature

To be added last:

2 cups finely sliced radish, **prepared as per first step**
2 cups finely sliced mushrooms
½ cup finely chopped parsley, or to taste
½ cup raisins

Garnish: 2 tbs. sunflower seeds (optional)
lettuce leaves, 6 large (optional)

Suggested dressing : Andalusian Dressing (page 68)

- To the sliced radish, add one tablespoon lemon juice (this turns the radish to a beautiful baby pink color) and a pinch of salt. Mix well to coat all over. Transfer to an airtight container and refrigerate.
- In a large bowl, combine the salad ingredients and refrigerate.
- **Just before serving:** Add the prepared radish, mushrooms, parsley and raisins to the salad ingredients. Add dressing and adjust seasoning to taste. Toss gently to combine the salad.
- At the very end, add the sunflower seeds (this helps retain its crunchiness).
- Arrange prepared salad on a bed of lettuce or serve as is.

Analysis per serving : (with sunflower seeds)

Calories (Kcal) : 291.7(308.8)   Total Fat (g) / % : 0.9/ 2.7 %(2.4 /6.8 %)

Carbohydrate (g) : 65.5 (66)   Saturated Fat (g) : 0.2 (0.3)

Dietary Fiber (g) : 3.7 (4)   Monounsaturated Fat (g) : 0.1 (0.4)

Protein (g) : 6.3 (6.9)   Polyunsaturated Fat (g) : 0.2 (1.2)

Sodium (mg) : 100 (100)   Cholesterol (mg) : 0 (0)

Fattoush (Lebanese Salad)   Serves : 6

I refuse to offer the original recipe because of its high fat content (about 1/2 cup of olive oil). This revised recipe retains the authentic taste, but minus the oil. The spice Sumac (see bottom of page for more information) enhances the flavor of the dressing and is a must.

Salad Ingredients:

2 cups shredded romaine lettuce or iceberg lettuce
1 medium seedless cucumber, cut into 1-inch cubes
1 green pepper, cut into 1-inch cube
2 tomatoes, cut into ½ -inch wedges
1 large red onion, halved and finely sliced, [soaked in 1 tbs. lemon
                                   juice and a pinch of salt.

Garnish: 2 pitas, **cut into ½-inch cubes & toasted in the oven**

Suggested dressing : Lebanese Dressing [page 70]

- In a large salad bowl, combine the "salad ingredients" and refrigerate.
- Just before serving, drizzle the dressing over the prepared salad.
- Toss well to combine. Just before serving, garnish with toasted pita croutons.

Analysis per serving:	
Calories (Kcal) : 100.6	Total Fat (g) / % : 0.6 / 4.7 %
Carbohydrate (g) : 21.6	Saturated Fat (g) : 0.1
Dietary Fiber (g) : 1.9	Monounsaturated Fat (g) : 0.1
Protein (g) : 3.6	Polyunsaturated Fat (g) : 0.3
Sodium (mg) : 300	Cholesterol (mg) : 0

Note: Information on Sumac**:
This spice is from the berries of a species of the sumac tree that have a sour lemony taste. To make Zahtar, a middle eastern spice blend
you need: *2 cups dried thyme,*
                1 cup sumac,
                1/2 cup toasted sesame seeds.
Sumac can be found in a ny Middle-Eastern grocery shop or health food store.

Bulgur & Chick Pea Salad — Serves : 6

An extremely nutritious and filling salad, especially if you are looking for a light meal. I sometimes use cooked lentils in place of chick peas and the salad tastes just as good. I use large size bulgur (can be found in health food shops) for this recipe as it has a crunchier and nuttier texture.

1 cup large size bulgur mixed in 2 cups hot water + 1/2 tsp. salt,
soaked for 30 minutes.

Salad Ingredients:

2 cups **cooked** chick peas, rinsed and drained
2 cups finely diced tomatoes
1 cup finely chopped green pepper
1 cup finely chopped red pepper
½ cup finely diced red onion
½ cup finely chopped parsley

Garnish : ¼ cup crumbled or diced feta cheese

Suggested dressing : Middle-Eastern Dressing (page 69)

- In a large bowl, combine the "salad ingredients" with the prepared Bulgur. Serve well chilled, after 2 hours.
- In a small bowl, combine the dressing ingredients. Pour the dressing over the prepared salad. Toss well to combine.
- Serve topped with feta cheese.

Analysis per serving : (with feta cheese)

Calories (Kcal) : 121.9 (134.3)	Total Fat (g) / % : 1.2 / 8.4 % (2.2 /14.2 %)
Carbohydrate (g) : 24.2 (24.4)	Saturated Fat (g) : 0.1 (0.8)
Dietary Fiber (g) : 5.1 (5.1)	Monounsaturated Fat (g) : 0.2 (0.5)
Protein (g) : 4.9 (5.6)	Polyunsaturated Fat (g) : 0.5 (0.6)
Sodium (mg) : 246 (298)	Cholesterol (mg) : 0 (4)

Herculean Greek Salad   Serves : 6

My love for this salad made me come up with this ultra low fat version. I hope you enjoy it as much as I do. Add a cup of cooked chick peas to make it a complete meal. This salad's savory flavor has muscle !

Salad Ingredients:

1 medium head of lettuce, **torn into bite-size portions, rinsed &**
soaked in cold water for ½ hour
1 medium seedless cucumber, ¼-inch slices
1 small red onion, halved & cut into thin slices **(soaked in ice cold water**
with a tbs. lemon juice for ½ hour & left to drain)
1 red **or** green pepper, julienned lengthwise
1 cup thinly sliced celery

Garnish & Decoration :

      5 - 6 tbs.roughly crumbled feta cheese
      ½ cup garlic flavored baked croutons, or as required

Suggested Dressing : Greek Dressing (see page: 69)

- Set lettuce to drain. Ensure it is totally dry before refrigerating.
- Arrange prepared lettuce in a large salad bowl or on a large platter.
- In a large bowl, combine the cucumber, prepared red onions, green peppers and celery with the dressing. Place them on top of the lettuce.
- Garnish with crumbled feta cheese, olives (optional) and baked croutons.

Analysis per serving :
Calories (Kcal) : 64.6	Total Fat (g) / % : 1.8 / 22.2 %
Carbohydrate (g) : 10.7	Saturated Fat (g) : 0.8
Dietary Fiber (g) : 3.3	Monounsaturated Fat (g) : 0.4
Protein (g) : 3.1	Polyunsaturated Fat (g) : 0.3
Sodium (mg) : 116	Cholesterol (mg) : 4

Spinach and Orange Salad   Serves : 6

If you want to be "strong to the finish" because you eat your spinach, this is the salad for you. I often make this when I don't feel like cooking. A perennial favourite of Popeye and many others. Not only is it packed with nutrition, it is tasty and visually appealing.

Salad Ingredients:

4 cups spinach leaves, stems removed, washed and left to drain
2 cups orange segments (oranges of your choice)
3 cups finely sliced mushrooms
1 cup finely sliced red or green pepper
1 cup finely sliced red onions, **mixed with 1 tbs. lemon juice, a pinch of salt & a pinch of sugar**

Garnish : 2 tbs. sliced almonds, toasted, optional

Suggested dressing: Poppy Seed Dressing [page 70]

- Transfer spinach to a large bowl, lined with paper towel, to absorb any remaining water. Transfer the cleaned and dry spinach to a salad bowl and refrigerate.
- Combine the remaining salad ingredients in another large bowl and refrigerate

Just before serving:
- Combine the spinach with the other salad ingredients. Toss well to combine.
- Garnish with toasted sliced almonds. Serve salad dressing on the side.

```
Analysis per serving : (with almonds)
Calories (Kcal) : 59.8 (77.2)        Total Fat (g) / % : 0.4 / 5.5 % (2/ 20.2% )
Carbohydrate (g) : 13.4 (14)         Saturated Fat (g): 0.1 (0.2)
Dietary Fiber (g) : 3.7 (4)          Monounsaturated Fat (g)  0 (1)
Protein (g) : 2.8 (3.4)              Polyunsaturated Fat (g) :0.2 (0.5)
Sodium (mg) : 32 (32)                Cholesterol (mg) : 0  (0)
```

Tropical Salad   Serves : 6

This exotic summer salad augments any table with its visual appeal. Always a favorite at festivities, every morsel bursts with fresh taste. The pineapple is a must in this salad for you to truly enjoy it.

¾ cup couscous
¾ cup hot water
1 tbs. fresh lemon juice
½ tsp. salt or to taste

Salad Ingredients:

2 cups fresh pineapple, cut into 1-inch chunks
2 mangoes, cut into 1-inch chunks
2 apples, cored and diced into 1-inch chunks
1 cup diced red pepper, cut into 1-inch pieces
1 cup diced green pepper, cut into 1-inch pieces
1 jicama, skinned and cut into 1-inch cubes

Suggested Dressing : Calypso Dressing (page 68)

- In a medium sized bowl, combine the couscous, hot water, lemon juice and salt. Stir until well combined. Set aside until all the water has been absorbed and then refrigerate.
- In another bowl, combine the "salad ingredients". Toss. Add dressing to taste and refrigerate.

Just before serving :
- Combine the chilled couscous, the prepared salad ingredients and dressing. Adjust dressing to taste.
- Stir well to combine. Serve immediately.

Analysis per serving :

Calories (Kcal) : 194.1	Total Fat (g) / % : 0.7 / 2.9 %
Carbohydrate (g) : 43.7	Saturated Fat (g) : 0.1
Dietary Fiber (g) : 5.4	Monounsaturated Fat (g) : 0.1
Protein (g) : 4.7	Polyunsaturated Fat (g) : 0.2
Sodium (mg) : 5	Cholesterol (mg) : 0

Andalusian Dressing   Makes: 1/2 cup

4 tbs. red wine vinegar
4 tbs. fresh lemon juice
2 tbs. honey or sweetener of your choice
salt **and** freshly ground black pepper to taste

- Combine and refrigerate in an airtight bottle.

Analysis per serving (per tablespoon):

Calories (Kcal) : 18.6	Total Fat (g) / % : 0 / 0 %
Carbohydrate (g) : 5.3	Saturated Fat (g) : 0
Dietary Fiber (g) : 0	Monounsaturated Fat (g) : 0
Protein (g) : 0	Polyunsaturated Fat (g) : 0
Sodium (mg) :0	Cholesterol (mg) : 0

Calypso Dressing   Makes: 1/2 cup

2 tbs. fresh lime juice
2 tbs. rice wine vinegar
2 tbs. lime rind or lemon rind
1 tbs. honey or sweetener of your choice
½ tsp. ground allspice
2 tbs. fresh, grated ginger
salt to taste
To be added just before serving: 2 tbs. dry toasted, broken peanuts

- Combine and refrigerate in an airtight bottle.

Analysis per serving (per tablespoon):

Calories (Kcal) : 22.6	Total Fat (g) / % : 1.1 / 39.4 %
Carbohydrate (g) : 3.2	Saturated Fat (g) : 0.2
Dietary Fiber (g) : 0.3	Monounsaturated Fat(g) : 0.6
Protein (g) : 0.6	Polyunsaturated Fat (g) : 0.4
Sodium (mg) : 1	Cholesterol (mg) : 0

Greek Salad Dressing   Makes : 1/2 cup

4 tbs. fresh lemon juice
2 tbs. flavored wine vinegar
2 tbs. nonfat yogurt
3 tbs. crushed feta cheese
2 tbs. grated parmesan cheese
1 tsp. honey or sweetener of your choice
2 - 3 medium sized garlic, crushed
2 tbs. freshly chopped oregano **or** 2 tsp. dry oregano
salt **and** freshly ground black pepper to taste

• Combine and refrigerate in an airtight bottle.

Analysis per serving (per tablespoon):

Calories (Kcal) : 13.7	Total Fat (g) / % : 0.6 / 36.1 %
Carbohydrate (g) : 1.6	Saturated Fat (g) : 0.4
Dietary Fiber (g) : 0	Monounsaturated Fat (g) : 0.1
Protein (g) : 0.8	Polyunsaturated Fat (g) : 0
Sodium (mg) : 34	Cholesterol (mg) : 2

Middle Eastern Dressing   Makes : 1/2 cup

2 tsp. **each** dried crushed oregano, basil, mint **and** sumac
6 tbs. fresh lemon juice
3 tbs. apple cider vinegar
2 tbs. honey or sweetener of your choice
salt **and** freshly ground black pepper to taste

• Combine and refrigerate in an airtight bottle.

Analysis per serving (per tablespoon):

Calories (Kcal) : 10.5	Total Fat (g) / % : 0 / 0 %
Carbohydrate (g) : 3.1	Saturated Fat (g) : 0
Dietary Fiber (g) : 0	Monounsaturated Fat (g) : 0
Protein (g) : 0	Polyunsaturated Fat (g) : 0
Sodium (mg) : 0	Cholesterol (mg) : 0

Poppy Seed Dressing   Makes : 1/2 cup

4 tbs. nonfat yogurt
2 tbs. fresh lemon juice
2 tbs. herb flavored vinegar
2 tbs. honey or sweetener of your choice
2 tbs. black poppy seeds
salt **and** freshly ground black pepper to taste

• Combine and refrigerate in an airtight bottle.

Analysis per serving (per tablespoon):
Calories (Kcal) : 33.3	Total Fat (g) / % : 1 / 24.6%
Carbohydrate (g) : 6	Saturated Fat (g) : 0.1
Dietary Fiber (g) : 0.7	Monounsaturated Fat (g) : 0.1
Protein (g) : 0.8	Polyunsaturated Fat (g) : 0.7
Sodium (mg) : 6	Cholesterol (mg) : 0

Lebanese Dressing   Makes: 1/2 cup

3 tbs. fresh lemon juice
2 tbs. honey or sweetener of your choice
1 tbs. crushed garlic
3 tbs. chopped Italian parsley
1 tbs. dried mint
1 tbs. ground sumac **(page 63 for more information)**
salt **and** freshly ground black pepper to taste

• Combine and refrigerate in an airtight bottle.

Analysis per serving (per tablespoon) :
Calories (Kcal) : 18.7	Total Fat (g) / % : 0/ 0.4%
Carbohydrate (g) : 5.1	Saturated Fat (g) : 0
Dietary Fiber (g) : 0.1	Monounsaturated Fat (g) : 0
Protein (g) : 0.1.	Polyunsaturated Fat (g) : 0
Sodium (mg) : 0	Cholesterol (mg) : 0

Malaysian Dressing

Makes : 1/2 cup

3 tbs. fresh lemon juice
3 tbs. rice vinegar
2 tbs. brown sugar
2 tsp. sweet chili sauce
2 tbs. chunky peanut butter
salt to taste

- Combine and refrigerate in an airtight bottle.

Analysis per serving (per tablespoon):

Calories (Kcal) : 34.7	Total Fat (g) / % : 2/47.7 %
Carbohydrate (g) : 4	Saturated Fat (g) : 0.4
Dietary Fiber (g) : 0.3	Monounsaturated Fat (g) : 1
Protein (g) : 1	Polyunsaturated Fat (g) : 0.6
Sodium (mg) : 21	Cholesterol (mg) : 0

Mexican Dressing

Makes: 1/2 cup

4 tbs. apple cider vinegar
2 tbs. fresh lemon juice, or to taste
2 tbs. honey or sweetener of your choice
1 tbs. crushed garlic
1 tbs. Mexican chili powder
½ tsp. crushed dry red chili flakes, or to taste

- Combine and refrigerate in an airtight bottle.

Analysis per serving (per tablespoon):

Calories (Kcal) : 22.7	Total Fat (g) / % : 0.2 / 5.8%
Carbohydrate (g) : 6	Saturated Fat (g) : 0
Dietary Fiber (g) : 0.4	Monounsaturated Fat (g) : 0
Protein (g) : 0.2	Polyunsaturated Fat (g) : 0
Sodium (mg) : 10	Cholesterol (mg) : 0

rice vinegar **&** apple cider vinegar
2 tbs. fresh lime juice , or to taste
2 tbs. honey or sweetener of your choiceto taste
½ tsp. ground all spice
2 tbs. black poppy seeds
crushed red chili pepper flakes, to taste (optional)
salt and freshly ground black pepper to taste

- Combine and refrigerate in an airtight bottle.

Analysis per serving (per tablespoon):	
Calories (Kcal) : 29.9	Total Fat (g) / % : 1 / 26.5 %
Carbohydrate (g) : 5.7	Saturated Fat (g) : 0.1
Dietary Fiber (g) : 0.7	Monounsaturated Fat (g) : 0.1
Protein (g) : 0.4	Polyunsaturated Fat (g) : 0.7
Sodium (mg) : 1	Cholesterol (mg) : 0

Strawberry Compote
Makes: 2 cups

I make large batches of the strawberry compote (when in season) and freeze them in small containers. It is excellent and manages to retain its freshness even after 6 months. For strawberry flavored yogurt, add strawberry compote to fresh nonfat yogurt.

4 cups fresh strawberries, washed and hulled
¼ cup sugar or sweetener of your choice

- Cut the cleaned strawberry into fairly small pieces.
- Combine the strawberry and sugar in a deep saucepan or skillet and cook on medium -high heat, for 10 minutes.
- Set aside to cool. Freeze in small, airtight containers .

Rice

Pasta

&

One Dish Meals

Mexican Rice   Serves: 6

This is a sure-fire, easy to make recipe. Once the vegetables are cut and ready, it takes about 10 minutes before I start the cooking process. Add a cup of cooked chick peas or cooked red beans, at the end of the cooking, to make this a complete meal.

1 tbs. canola oil
1 cup finely chopped onions
2 tbs. crushed garlic
1 cup chopped celery
2 cups long grain rice **or** converted rice
4 cups water
1 cup frozen corn kernels
1 cup tomato paste
¾ tsp. salt , or to taste
1 tbs. cumin powder
½ tsp. chili powder
1 tbs. canned, chopped jalapeño peppers (page 90)

Garnish: ½ cup **each** chopped green pepper **and** coriander leaves

- Preheat oven to 375°F.
- Heat the oil in a large non-stick Dutch oven or saucepan, over medium heat and sauté onions (with a pinch of salt) until golden brown. Add the garlic and sauté for 5 seconds. Transfer to an ovenproof casserole. Add the remaining ingredients.
- Stir and **bake covered** in a preheated oven for 35 to 40 minutes or, until the rice is cooked. Remove from oven. Fluff the rice with a fork. Garnish and serve hot.

Analysis per serving:
Calories (Kcal) : 260.2	Total Fat (g) / % : 3 / 10 %
Carbohydrate (g) : 57.6	Saturated Fat (g) : 0.3
Dietary Fiber (g) : 3.7	Monounsaturated Fat (g) : 1.5
Protein (g) : 3.2	Polyunsaturated Fat (g) : 1
Sodium (mg) : 417	Cholesterol (mg) : 0

Masala Khichari (Rice and Lentil Pilaf)

Serves : 6

A fragrant and light East-Indian pilaf, this rice dish can hold its own with just a couple of vegetable dishes to make a satisfying meal.

1 cup Masoor Dal (red lentils), washed and set aside to drain
1 cup Basmati Rice, washed and set aside to drain
1 tbs. canola oil
2 tsp. cumin seeds
1 tsp. black peppercorns
1 cup finely diced onions
2 tsp. crushed garlic
2 tsp. grated ginger
4 bay leaves
½ tsp. chili powder, or to taste
4 cups hot water
¾ tsp. salt, or to taste

Garnish :   **¼ cup fried onions, optional**
2 tbs. toasted, broken cashews
¼ cup chopped fresh coriander leaves, for garnish

- Preheat oven to 350°F.
- Heat the oil in a deep nonstick skillet over medium-high heat. Add the cumin seeds, peppercorns, onions (with a pinch of salt) and sauté until translucent. Add the spices and sauté for 10 seconds. Add the rice and lentils and stir thoroughly to combine, for 5 minutes.
- Transfer to an ovenproof casserole. Add water and salt. Stir. Bake **covered** for 25 minutes.
- Reduce the oven heat to 250° F. **Remove cover.**
- Fluff rice with a fork and return to bake **uncovered,** for another 20 minutes or until all the water has been absorbed. Remove casserole from oven.
- Garnish with toasted cashews, fried onions and chopped coriander.
- Serve hot. Goes well with any vegetable curry especially the Pumpkin Patchadi.

Analysis per serving:
Calories (Kcal) : 262.9
Carbohydrate (g) : 45.1
Dietary Fiber (g) : 10.6
Protein (g) : 11.9
Sodium (mg) : 104

Total Fat (g) / % : 4.1 / 14 %
Saturated Fat (g) : 0.5
Monounsaturated Fat (g) : 2.2
Polyunsaturated Fat (g) : 1.1
Cholesterol (mg) : 0

EVERYTHING UNDER CONTROL !

Vegetable Biryani (Fried Rice)   Serves : 6

Once the ingredients have been assembled, this mouthwatering biryani can be made with minimal effort. When the baking starts, so does the salivating. This dish engulfs the entire house with ex otic aromas that emanate from its spices. Be prepared to dish out seconds and thirds.

2 medium sized potatoes with skin, cleaned and quartered
1 tbs. canola oil to brown the quartered potatoes

1 tbs. canola oil +1 tsp. butter
1 tbs. cumin seeds
1 cup finely diced onions
2 tsp. grated ginger
2 tsp. crushed garlic
2 green chilies, chopped fine
4, 1-inch cinnamon sticks
4 cloves
4 whole cardamom with skin
1 cup diced carrots
1 cup green beans, 1-inch pieces
1 cup cauliflower florets, large pieces
1 cup raw Basmati rice, rinsed and set to drain
1 ¾ cup water
¾ tsp. salt, or to taste
1 cup frozen peas
1 large red pepper, diced
1 medium green pepper, diced
½ cup raisins
¼ cup fresh, chopped coriander
3 tbs. broken cashews, **toasted till golden brown**

- Preheat oven to 375°F.
- Heat 1 tbs. oil in a large non-stick skillet over medium heat and sauté the diced potatoes until golden brown. Remove browned potatoes from the skillet and set aside.
- Add the oil and butter to the same skillet. Add the cumin seeds, onions (with a pinch of salt) and sauté until golden brown. Add the

ginger, garlic, green chilies and the remaining spices and sauté for 10 seconds. Transfer to a large ovenproof casserole or roast pan.

- Add the prepared potatoes, carrots, beans, cauliflower, drained rice, water and salt. Stir well to mix.
- Bake **covered** for 30 minutes. Remove cover. Fluff rice. Add the green peas, the red and green peppers and raisins. Stir gently to combine.
- Bake **uncovered** for 15 minutes.
- Serve hot garnished with toasted cashews (optional) and chopped coriander leaves. Serve with fruit raita.

Analysis per serving (with cashews) :

Calories (Kcal) : 271.2 (294.6)	Total Fat (g) / % : 5.8 / 18.9 % (1.3 / 23.2 %).
Carbohydrate (g) : 50.4 (51.6)	Saturated Fat (g) : 0.9
Dietary Fiber (g) : 4.8 (4.9)	Monounsaturated Fat (g) : 3.0
Protein (g) : 5.9 (6.5)	Polyunsaturated Fat (g) : 1.6
Sodium (mg) : 144 (145)	cholesterol (mg) : 2

Variation

To cook Basmati Rice over stove top:

Use the ratio : 1 cup rice to 1 ¾ cups water.

To cook Basmati Rice in the Microwave Oven

Using the ratio - 1 cup rice to 1¾ cups water, cook the rice, uncovered, to prevent it from softening excessively.

To make a simple Vegetable Pilaf with 1 cup raw rice :

- ♥ *Cook and cool required amount of Basmati rice.*
- ♥ *Using a deep, large nonstick skillet, sauté 1 cup finely diced onion in a tbs. of canola oil . Add 3/4 tsp. garam masala. Sauté for a few seconds.*
- ♥ *Add 2 cups mixed steamed vegetables of your choice. Add the cooked and cooled rice to the vegetable mixture. Stir until well combined. Serve hot with fruit raita (Page : 39)*

78

David's High Energy Lasagna   Serves : 8

This lasagna is the perennial favorite of my body-building cousin David, who can demolish half of it in one sitting, . You can make it as interesting as you want it to be. The addition of apples helps cut down on the strong tomato taste. The tofu blends beautifully with the other ingredients and gives it a rich taste.

10 - 12 cooked lasagna noodles (instructions as per package)

or

10 - 12 oven ready lasagna noodles (needs no pre-cooking)

For the Sauce:

1 tsp. olive oil
½ cup finely chopped onions + a pinch of salt
2 tbs. crushed garlic
1 tbs. Italian seasoning
½ tsp. freshly ground black pepper, or to taste
1 tbs. brown sugar or sweetener of your choice
2 cups canned crushed tomatoes **mixed** with 2 cups water
½ tsp. salt, or to taste

Vegetable Mixture: (all vegetables to be sliced thin):

½ cup *each* zucchini, mushrooms, green pepper and carrots
1 large apple, cored and sliced thin

Cheese Mixture: to be combined, in a medium sized bowl

¼ cup finely chopped fresh parsley
2 cups dry, lowfat cottage cheese
1 cup Silken Tofu or soft Tofu
¾ cup grated mozzarella cheese (7%)

Topping:

4 tbs. grated parmesan cheese
¼ cup fresh breadcrumbs

To prepare the tomato sauce :

- Heat oil in deep nonstick skillet over medium-high heat and sauté the onions (with a pinch of salt) until golden brown. Add garlic, the remaining spices and sugar and sauté for 10 seconds.
- Stir in the crushed tomatoes and water. Cook, covered, on medium heat, for 10 minutes,
- Lower heat and keep sauce warm for the layering.

Assembling / Layering the lasagna :

- Preheat oven to 375°F. Grease a 9 x 13-inch baking dish. Set aside.
    Spread ½ the prepared tomato sauce in the prepared baking dish.
    Cover it with a layer of the lasagna noodles.
    Spread ½ the prepared vegetables mixture in a single layer.
    Spread ½ of the cheese mixture.
    Cover it with the remaining lasagna noodles.
    Spread the remaining cheese mixture.
    Spread the remaining vegetable mixture.
    Finish with the remaining tomato sauce.
    Sprinkle with fresh bread crumbs and grated parmesan cheese.

The final task:

- Bake, **covered,** for 45 minutes.
- Serve lasagna warm after 20 minutes. Serve with a light salad on the side.

Analysis per serving :
Calories (Kcal) : 544.6   Total Fat (g) / % : 7.1 / 11.7 %
Carbohydrate (g) : 91.3   Saturated Fat (g) : 2.6
Dietary Fiber (g) : 4.4   Monounsaturated Fat (g) : 1.9
Protein (g) : 28.0   Polyunsaturated Fat (g) : 1.7
Sodium (mg) : 503   Cholesterol (mg) : 10

Hors d'oeuvres
Map for overleaf photo

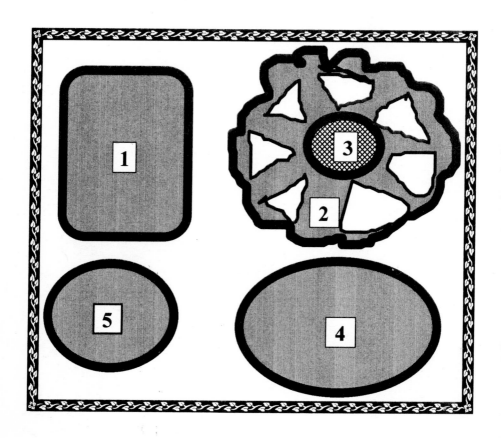

1. Hockey Puck Latkes (Page: 21)

2. Canadian Baked Samosas (Page: 18)

3. Date Chutney (Page: 37)

4. Masala Vadas (Page: 28)

5. Cheese & Carrot Rolls (Page: 22)

Dips, Sauces & Chutneys
Map for overleaf photo

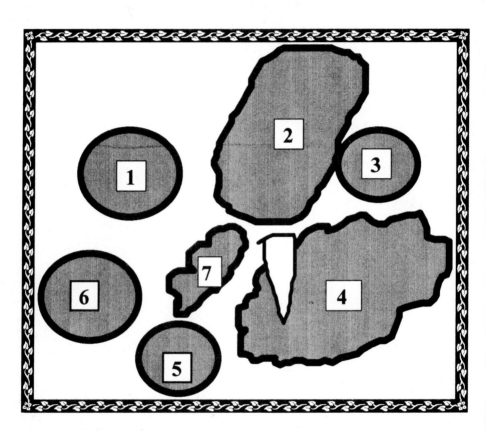

1. Verdant Pesto (Page: 41)

2. Chuckie's Cornmeal Bread (Page: 125)

3. Strawberry Compote (Page: 72)

4. Tropical Salsa Cruda (Page: 36)

5. Decadent Date Chutney (Page: 37)

6. Cranberry Fruit Chutney (Page: 34)

7. Challah (Page: 127)

Hearty Soups
Map for overleaf photo

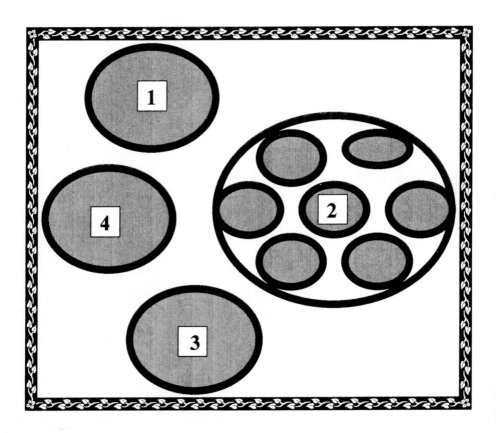

1. Pasta E Fagioli (Page: 51)

2. Mexicasa Corn Muffins (Page: 121)

3. Potato and Barley Soup (Page: 45)

4. Manchurian Soup (Page : 53)

Salads & Dressings
Map for overleaf photo

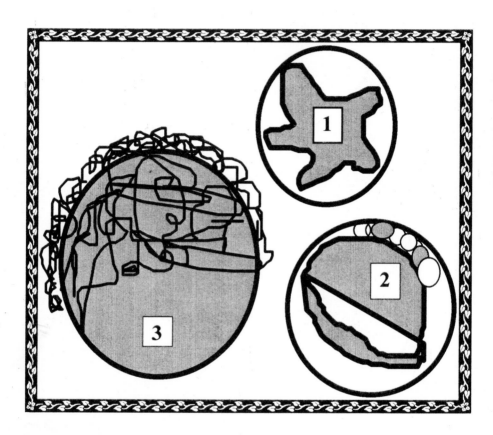

1. The McBean Salad (Page: 59)

2. McBean Salad served in a Pita

3. Andalusian Salad (Page: 61)

Rice, Pasta & One Dish Meals
Map for overleaf photo

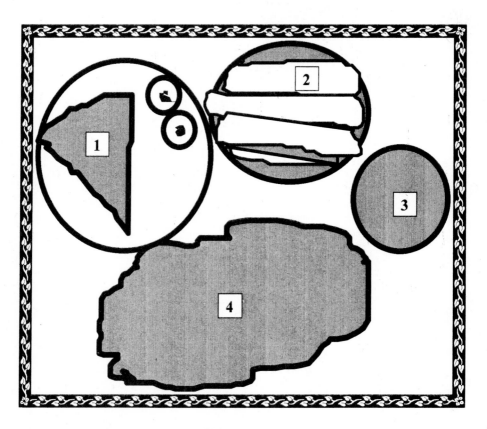

1. Athenian Pie (Page: 81)

2. Volcanic Enchiladas (Page: 89)

3. Powdered Sumac (a spice) (Page: 63)

4. Szechwan Rice (Page: 97)

Vegetable Ecstasies
Map for overleaf photo

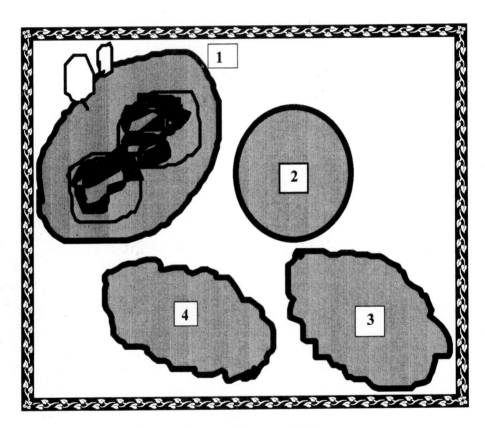

1. Vegetarian Sloppy Joes (Page: 116)

2. Sicilian Bean Casserole (Page: 111)

3. Alu Gobi (Page: 103)

4. Mattar Paneer (Page: 109)

Muffins, Breads, Flatbreads & More
Map for overleaf photo

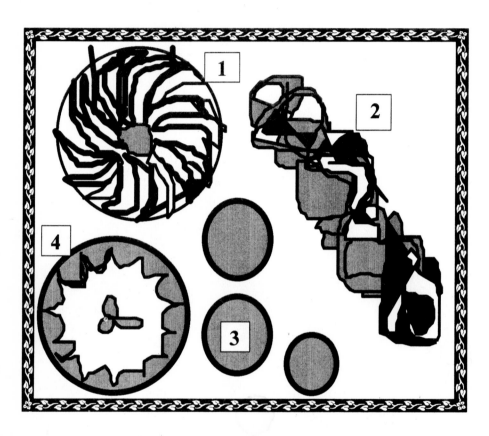

1. Mexican Apple & Cheddar Cake (Page: 138)

2. Challah (Page: 127)

3. Hawaiian Fruit Muffins (Page: 118)

4. AnyBerry Cheesecake (Page: 131)

Athenian Pie   Serves : 6

Make sure you eat something before baking this pie. Otherwise you may devour the whole pie before the rest of your family gets to it. If there are leftovers, though, I use them the next day as sandwich filling for a nutritious light meal.

Crust ingredients :
¾ cup fresh, whole-wheat bread crumbs
4 tbs. quick cooking oats
1 tsp. Italian seasoning
salt and pepper, to taste
lowfat margarine for greasing pie plate

Pie filling ingredients:
1 package frozen, chopped spinach, **thawed and squeezed dry**
½ cup nonfat yogurt
4 tbs. crumbled feta cheese
1 cup nonfat, dry cottage cheese **or** 1 cup low-fat ricotta cheese
1 tbs. minced garlic
¼ cup fresh bread crumbs
1 tsp. dried oregano
¼ tsp. ground cinnamon
¼ tsp. freshly ground nutmeg

For final mixing: 8 egg-whites, **well beaten to a soft peak**

- Preheat oven to 400°F.
- Coat a 9-inch pie plate or 8-inch springform pan with margarine.
- In a small bowl, combine the "crust ingredients". Line the greased pie plate or pan with the prepared pie crust (it will resemble a dry crust).
- In a large bowl, combine the spinach with the remaining "pie filling ingredients". Finally, fold in the beaten egg-whites. Pour into the prepared pie plate.
- Bake for 30 minutes or until a knife inserted in the center comes out clean.
- Goes well with Tropical Salsa Cruda or nonfat sour cream.

Analysis per serving:
Calories (Kcal) : 126.8
Carbohydrate (g) : 13.1
Dietary Fiber (g) : 1.5
Protein (g) : 14.9
Sodium (mg) : 234

Total Fat (g) / % : 1.8 / 12.6 %
Saturated Fat (g) : 0.9
Monounsaturated Fat (g) : 0.5
Polyunsaturated Fat (g) : 0.2
Cholesterol (mg) : 5

Other ideas for the Athenian Pie :

Use 6 cups of cleaned, freshly chopped and firmly packed fresh Spinach or fresh Swiss chard , in the place of the frozen spinach in the Athenian Pie.

When using fresh spinach or Swiss chard:

♥ *Stove top method:* Steam the chopped spinach or swiss chard sprinkled with a few drops of water, in a large pot, covered, for 6 - 8 minutes, on medium-high.

or

Microwave method: Steam in a microwave-ovenproof container for 7 minutes, on high, covered.

♥ Set aside to drain . Cool it lightly before using the freshly cooked Spinach or Swiss chard. Then follow the recipe for the Athenian Pie. It tastes just as good, if not better.

Pad Thai   Serves: 6

This much sought after Thai recipe has gone through a lot of changes and testing to perfect the taste without losing its authenticity. Connoisseurs of Pad Thai insist that this is the best vegetarian version they have tasted. Fresh Lime augments this recipe and is a must.

¾ package dried, flat, medium sized rice noodles, **washed and soaked in hot water for 30 minutes (see notes at end of recipe)**
2 tbs. canola oil
1 cup finely diced onion
1 tbs. grated ginger
2 tbs. crushed garlic
a few pieces lemon grass, cut into fine strips (optional)
1 cup finely julienned carrots, **steamed**
1 cup long beans, cut into 2-inch pieces, **blanched**
1 cup frozen green peas
½ cup finely julienned green pepper
½ cup finely julienned red pepper
1 cup thinly sliced strips of firm tofu

For the sauce:
1 - 2 tbs. ketchup, or to taste
1 - 2 tbs. tamarind paste **or** 5 tbs. fresh lime juice
4 tbs. rice wine vinegar
2 tbs. soya sauce, low sodium
1 tbs. brown sugar or sweetener of your choice
1 - 2 tbs. sweet chili sauce, or to taste
salt, ground black pepper **and** crushed red pepper flakes, to taste

For the omelet : **2** egg-whites beaten with a tbs. of water, a pinch of salt and crushed red pepper

For the garnish:
2 cups fresh bean sprouts
1 lime, cut into wedges
1 tbs. roasted peanuts, coarsely chopped, (optional)
½ cup finely chopped coriander leaves
½ cup finely chopped green onions

- Drain soaked noodles. Set aside.
- Combine the sauce ingredients in a small bowl. Set aside.
- Heat oil in a large, deep nonstick skillet or wok over medium heat and sauté the onions (with a pinch of salt) until golden brown. Add the ginger, garlic and lemon grass. Sauté for a few seconds. Add the vegetables and tofu strips and stir-fry for 4 minutes.
- Add the sauce and bring it to a boil. Add the soaked and drained noodles. Add salt and adjust seasoning to taste. Stir well to combine.
- Cook**(see notes at bottom of page) covered for 10 - 15 minutes or until heated through, on medium heat. Set aside,

To make the omelet:

- In a small frying pan, make an omelet with the beaten egg. When cool, roll the omelet into a tight roll and cut it into thin strips. Set aside

How to serve Pad Thai :

- Discard the lemon grass strips.
- Toss in the bean sprouts at the very end and transfer the prepared Pad Thai to a serving platter.
- Garnish with chopped peanuts, coriander leaves, omelet strips, lime wedges and green onions. Serve hot.

Analysis per serving: (with peanuts)	
Calories (Kcal) : 327 (335.9)	Total Fat (g) / % : 8.3 / 21.6 % (9.0/23.%)
Carbohydrate (g) : 48.4 (48.7)	Saturated Fat (g) : 1.1 (1.2)
Dietary Fiber (g) : 12.9 (13.0)	Monounsaturated Fat (g) : 3.4 (3.8)
Protein (g) : 18.8 (19.2)	Polyunsaturated Fat (g) : 2.9 (3.2)
Sodium (mg) : 519 (532)	Cholesterol (mg) : 0 (0)

Notes on cooking Rice Noodles or Rice Vermicelli

**The flat noodles used in the Pad Thai are already processed and take very little time to cook, once soaked.*
Keep a watchful eye while heating the Pad Thai to prevent overcooked noodles. I always stay in the kitchen area for the last few steps of the Pad Thai to avoid disasters.

Veggie Loaf or Patties   Serves : 6

The initial question that crosses each of my student's minds when they are introduced to this recipe is: "If something is this simple to make, how is it going to taste ?". But once the finished recipe is being sampled, the silence followed by the Oohs and Aah's are answer enough for me. Add steamed asparagus, when in season, for a variation.

Cooked Loaf Ingredients:
½ cup **RAW** lentils, **cooked and drained** (yellow mung)
2 large potatoes, **cooked and slightly broken up**

Raw Loaf Ingredients:
½ cup finely chopped onions or finely chopped green onions
2 cups coarsely grated carrots
2 cups sliced mushrooms
1 cup finely diced red **or** green pepper
½ tsp. chili powder, or to taste
1 tbs. coriander powder
2 tsp. cumin powder
1 tbs. ground allspice
¾ tsp. salt, or to taste
1 cup rolled oats **or** quick cooking oats **or** oatmeal
4 tbs. sunflower seeds (optional)
½ cup finely chopped parsley or coriander leaves

Loaf Topping : 4 tsp. toasted sesame seeds

- Preheat oven to 350°F. Lightly grease a large loaf pan.
- In a large bowl, combine the "cooked loaf ingredients" with the "raw loaf ingredients". Adjust seasoning to taste.
- Pack the loaf mixture into the prepared loaf pan. Sprinkle sesame seeds on top. Press them in lightly.
- Bake 30 minutes, **covered.**
- Remove cover. Bake for **another 20 minutes** until the top of loaf is golden brown.
- Let the loaf stand for about 10 minutes before serving.
- Unmold the loaf onto a serving platter and decorate surrounded by

alfalfa sprouts, sliced tomatoes, or any other colorful vegetable of your choice.

- Serve with Tropical Salsa Cruda or sauce of your choice.

For Vegetable Patties:

- Follow the procedure as for loaf. Instead of packing them into a loaf pan, form into patties, using a bit of flour to help shape them. Refrigerate for a couple of hours. Heat frypan. Spray pan with a cooking spray or grease it lightly. Cook patties on both sides until golden.
- Serve hot on a bun with lettuce and vegetables of your choice.

Analysis per serving (with sunflower seeds) :
Calories (Kcal) : 142 (176.2)   Total Fat (g) / % : 2.3 / 14.2% (5.3 / 25.8%)
Carbohydrate (g) : 25.8 (26.9)   Saturated Fat (g) : 0.4 (0.7)
Dietary Fiber (g) : 5.3 (5.9)   Monounsaturated Fat (g) : 0.7 (1.3)
Protein (g) : 6.1 (7.5)   Polyunsaturated Fat (g) : 1 (2.9)
Sodium (mg) : 70 (70)   Cholesterol (mg) : 0 (0)

Kasha &Potato Crust Quiche   Serves : 6

This low-fat foolproof version is a perfect addition to a brunch, high tea, lunch or a cozy dinner. The flaky crust can be made the day before, and the filling on the day you are making the quiche, since it takes very little time. The smell of the tarragon, eggs and vegetables makes this a mouth watering experience.

For the crust:

2 -3 large potatoes, scrubbed, peeled, **cooked and mashed**
¼ cup buckwheat groats, **soaked in 1/4 cup warm, skim milk**
1 tbs. olive oil
½ tsp. **each** salt, crushed red chili flakes **and** dill weed
½ cup finely julienned red onion
vegetable cooking spray to grease the pan + top of the crust

For the Cheese Filling : (combine and set aside)

½ cup grated lowfat cheddar cheese
½ cup grated lowfat Swiss cheese

For the Vegetable Filling :

1 cup broccoli florets, **steamed until soft**
1 cup finely sliced mushrooms

For the egg filling : (combine and have ready)

6 egg-whites, **well beaten to a soft peak**
1 cup nonfat yogurt
4 tbs. all-purpose flour
1 tsp. **each** fresh **or** ¼ tsp. **each** dried spices such as thyme,
                              tarragon & oregano

Garnish : ½ tsp. crushed chili flakes, or to taste

- Preheat oven to 375°F. Lightly grease a 10-inch springform pan.
- In a medium sized bowl, combine "for the crust" ingredients. Spread the prepared crust to cover the greased springform pan. Spray the top of the crust very lightly with cooking spray and bake for 20 - 25 minutes.

- Remove from oven. Spread the prepared "Cheese Filling" over the baked crust.
- Lay the prepared "Vegetable Filling" over the cheese layer.
- Pour the egg filling over the vegetable layer, finishing with a garnish of red chili flakes.
- Bake at 375^0 F for 35 - 40 minutes or until firm. Cool for 10 minutes, to set, before serving.

Analysis per serving:

Calories (Kcal) : 201.1	Total Fat (g) / % : 3.9 / 18.1 %
Carbohydrate (g) : 25.5	Saturated Fat (g) : 1.2
Dietary Fiber (g) : 2.1	Monounsaturated Fat (g) : 2.1
Protein (g) : 14.6	Polyunsaturated Fat (g) : 0.4
Sodium (mg) : 358	Cholesterol (mg) : 6

Volcanic Enchiladas   Makes: 12

The youngest fan of this recipe is my 9 year old niece, Pooja from New Zealand, who claims that " This is the best food I've had in this whole wide world ". A sure to please recipe for food lovers of all ages. The bean and cheese filling is so smooth that it glides down your throat like a spoonful of jello. I derive great satisfaction from the excited responses to this recipe.

Bean and Cheese Filling
2 cups **cooked** red kidney beans, **cooled & mashed lightly**
1 cup low-fat (5%) ricotta cheese
½ to ¾ cup grated low-fat cheddar cheese

For the Sauce:
1 tsp. canola oil
1 cup finely diced onions
2 tbs. crushed garlic
1 tsp. dried oregano
1 tbs. canned jalapeño peppers, or to taste (see next page)
1 tbs. red wine vinegar
½ tsp. ground cinnamon
2 cups canned crushed tomatoes + 2 cups water
¼ cup tomato paste
¾ tsp. salt, or to taste
1 cup minced red or green peppers
¼ cup freshly chopped coriander leaves
For assembling : 12 large flour tortillas

- Preheat oven to 350°F. Lightly grease two 9x13-inch baking pans. Set aside.
- In a medium-sized bowl, combine the cooked and mashed beans, ricotta cheese and ¾ of the cheddar cheese. Set aside.

To prepare the tomato sauce:
- Heat oil in a deep skillet over medium-high heat and sauté the onions (with a pinch of salt) until golden brown. Add the garlic and the remaining spices and sauté for 5 seconds.
- Add the crushed tomatoes, water and tomato paste, Stir. Bring the

89

sauce to a rolling boil. Add the green peppers and coriander leaves and let the sauce cook for 3 minutes. Remove from heat. Spread a thin layer of this sauce in the prepared baking pan.

Assembling the Enchiladas : [It might be a slightly messy operation]
- Take one tortilla. Dip both sides into the prepared tomato sauce to soften the tortilla. Lay it on a plate and place 2-3 heaping tablespoons of the prepared "Bean & Cheese Filling" at one end of the sauce coated tortilla. Roll the filled tortilla to resemble a big cigar. Place seam side down in the prepared baking dish.
- Repeat until all the tortillas and filling are used up.
- You should have some of the tomato sauce left over after dipping the tortillas. If the remaining sauce is too thick, then thin it with ¼ cup water and spoon evenly over the prepared enchiladas.
- Sprinkle remainder of the cheddar cheese over the enchiladas. Cover with aluminum foil and bake in a preheated oven for 20 minutes.

Analysis per serving :	
Calories (Kcal) : 287.8	Total Fat (g) / % : 5.4 / 16.9 %
Carbohydrate (g) : 45.5	Saturated Fat (g) : 1.0
Dietary Fiber (g) : 10	Monounsaturated Fat (g) : 1.9
Protein (g) : 14.1	Polyunsaturated Fat (g) : 1.4
Sodium (mg) : 477	Cholesterol (mg) : 7

Note: Home made Canned Jalapeño Peppers

Almost all Mexican recipes require jalapeños. Buying canned jalapeños could prove to be costly. Here's an inexpensive way to make your own home-made canned jalapeños - it takes only 10 minutes for the whole task.

Use fresh plump jalapeños. Wash and dry them. Use rubber gloves before you start cutting the jalapeños (as a precautionary step to avoid hands from getting in contact with your eyes) . Remove stem, cut jalapeños into thin slices, seeds included. Transfer to a deep pan and cover cut jalapeños with apple cider vinegar, a pinch of salt and a teaspoon of sugar. Cook on medium-high heat and when it comes to a rolling boil, remove from heat. When cool, transfer to airtight jars . Refrigerate and enjoy the fruits or shall I say vegetables of your labor.

Aztec Corn Casserole   Serves: 6

This casserole can be made ahead of time and reheated when you are ready to eat it. The spices tend to release their flavor and taste better the next day. This dish spices up any gathering. One mouthful, and you'll think you have been whisked away to Mexico.

Vegetable Filling :
2 tsp. canola oil
1 cup finely diced onions
1 tbs. crushed garlic
2 tsp. **each** dried oregano **and** ground cumin
½ tsp. chili powder
3 cups chopped tomatoes
2 tbs. brown sugar
3 tbs. **each** lemon juice **and** red wine vinegar
½ tsp. salt, or to taste
1 cup finely diced green **or** red peppers
¼ cup finely chopped coriander leaves

Corn Filling :
4 cups water
2 cups fresh or canned corn kernels, drained
2 cups cornmeal
¼ tsp. **each** salt **and** crushed chili pepper

Cheese Layer:
1 cup grated low-fat cheddar cheese
1 tbs. canned, sliced, red chili peppers, or to taste

- Grease a bundt pan **or** 10 -inch springform baking pan. Set aside.
- **Vegetable Filling** : Heat oil in a deep nonstick skillet over medium-high heat and sauté the onions (with a pinch of salt) until golden brown.. Add the garlic and remaining spices and sauté for 10 seconds.Add the tomatoes, brown sugar, lemon juice, red wine vinegar and salt. Stir. Cover and cook for 15 minutes. Remove the lid. Add the green or red pepper and coriander leaves. Stir well to combine. Cook until almost all the water is absorbed.

- **Corn filling** : In a large saucepan over medium-high heat bring the water with salt, crushed chili pepper and corn kernels to a rolling boil. Lower the heat. Add the cornmeal in a steady flow, whisking it in gently to avoid lumping. Stir constantly until the mixture gets thick, about 10 minutes. Cover and cook on low heat for 10 minutes.

- **Layering and Baking** : Spread half the prepared corn filling in the bundt pan. Cover it with half the tomato mixture and spread ¾ of the cheese and red chili peppers. Finish up with the remaining corn mixture, followed by the tomato mixture and ending with the remaining cheese. Bake at 350°F for 40 minutes. Let it set for 10 minutes before serving. Goes well with a light salad.

Analysis per serving:

Calories (Kcal) : 327.0	Total Fat (g) / % : 4.4 / 12.4 %
Carbohydrate (g) : 58.6	Saturated Fat (g) : 1.2
Dietary Fiber (g) : 6.5	Monounsaturated Fat (g) : 1.7
Protein (g) : 11.5	Polyunsaturated Fat (g) : 1.2
Sodium (mg) : 496	Cholesterol (mg) : 4

Broccoli Risotto Torte
with Tomato Sauce   Serves : 10

This Italian rice dish has earned a lot of praise and some of my students don't have the patience to wait for the tomato sauce to be made. I love it when it's piping hot. I serve it with Tropical Salsa Cruda (page 36) when I don't feel like making the tomato sauce.

2 cups risotto rice (ARBORIO), to be cooked first in 4 cups water
1 tbs. olive oil
1 cup finely chopped onion
1 tbs. crushed garlic
4 cups broccoli, **cut into very small florets**
2 cups finely diced green **or** red pepper
1 tsp. crushed red pepper flakes, or to taste
salt and crushed black pepper, to taste
1 cup grated parmesan or as desired
6 egg-whites, **well beaten** + 1 yolk
Oil for greasing pan
For Decoration : sliced tomatoes, sliced cucumber

- Cook the arborio rice in 4 cups water until soft. Set it aside.
- Preheat oven to 350°F. Grease a 12-inch springform pan
- Heat oil in deep skillet over medium-high heat and sauté the onions (with a pinch of salt) until translucent. Add the garlic, broccoli, green or red pepper, crushed red pepper, salt, pepper and ¼ **cup water**. Stir. Cover and cook for 10 minutes or until vegetables are fairly soft.
- Add the cooked rice with whatever liquid is left in it. Stir thoroughly ensuring there are no lumps. Adjust seasoning to taste. Stir in the grated parmesan cheese and the yolk **(if you are using it)**.
- Allow the rice mixture to cool for 15 minutes.
- In the meantime, beat the whites to a soft peak. Carefully fold into the rice mixture. Spoon the egg/rice mixture into the greased pan.
- Bake for an hour or until golden brown. It will be slightly wobbly in the centre. Allow the torte to cool in the tin.
- Run a knife around the edge of the tin and gently transfer it to a serving plate. Garnish with sliced tomato and chopped parsley.

Tomato Sauce

1 tsp. olive oil
1 cup diced onion
1 tbs. crushed garlic
1 tbs. brown sugar or sweetener of your choice
1 tsp. paprika
6 tbs. fresh herbs (basil, parsley, rosemary, marjoram) **or**
                 2 tbs. Italian seasoning
6 cups fresh diced tomatoes
salt and freshly crushed black pepper, to taste
1 cup diced red pepper

- Heat the oil in a large skillet over medium-high heat. Add the onions (with a pinch of salt) and sauté until translucent. Add the garlic, brown sugar, paprika and herbs and sauté for a minute.
- Add the tomatoes; salt and pepper. Stir thoroughly, bringing it to a gentle boil. Lower heat and cook, covered, for 15 minutes. Add the red pepper and cook for a 3 minutes. The sauce should be thick and pulpy. If it is too thin, cook uncovered for a few minutes, until thick. You can puree this, if need be or serve as is with the risotto torte.

Analysis per serving (analysis includes tomato sauce):

Calories (Kcal) : 263.3	Total Fat (g) / % : 5.4 / 18.1 %
Carbohydrate (g) : 43	Saturated Fat (g) : 2
Dietary Fiber (g) : 4.2	Monounsaturated Fat (g) : 2.3
Protein (g) : 11.9	Polyunsaturated Fat (g) : 0.6
Sodium (mg) : 329	Cholesterol (mg) : 28

Notes on Arborio Rice

Arborio Rice, an Italian rice, when cooked is noted for its creamy texture. If you trying substituting other rice varieties for the Broccoli Risotto Torte or Rice pudding you will not achieve the desired results. Arborio rice should be available at your local supermarket or grocery stores.

Usha's Upma (Cream of Wheat Pilaf)   Serves : 6

I could eat UPMA (pronounced OOPMA) every day of the week. This recipe has picked up a lot of fans along the way. A few hours before I gave birth to my daughter, Divya, I had severe cravings for Upma. I made a large batch and refused to share it with anyone. That's how passionate I can get about this dish. My ideal meal, I would say, is Upma with the Pumpkin Patchadi.

**2 cups semolina (cream of wheat), dry toasted, on stove top over
medium-high heat, for 10 minutes**

1 tsp. ghee [melted butter]
1 tbs. canola oil
1 tbs. mustard seeds
1 tbs. urad dal [white lentils]
1 tbs. yellow split peas
1 cup finely diced onion
1 tbs. finely minced ginger
2 - 3 finely chopped green chilies **or** to taste
1 tsp. garam masala (see page: 96 for recipe)
1 cup **each** finely diced carrots **and** fresh green beans
1 cup **each** frozen corn kernels **and** frozen green peas
4 cups water
¾ - 1 tsp. salt , or to taste
1 cup finely diced green or red pepper
3 tbs. finely chopped coriander leaves

- Heat the ghee and oil in a large nonstick Dutch oven over medium heat. Add mustard seeds, white lentils and split peas. When the mustard seed starts spluttering and the lentils have turned a golden red color, add the onions, minced ginger and chopped green chilies and sauté for 4 minutes. Add the vegetables and toss well to coat.
- Add the salt and water to the vegetables and let it come to a rolling boil. When vegetables are cooked [it should take 8 - 10 minutes after the water starts boiling] **turn the heat to low** to avoid the bubbling water from splashing on your hands.
- Have a whisk handy and incorporate the toasted semolina into the boiling water, in a steady stream to avoid lumping.

- Cover and cook until all the water is absorbed, over low heat, about 10 minutes. This is a fairly dry dish. Towards the end, stir in the green or red peppers together with the coriander leaves. Cover and cook for a further 5 minutes.
- Serve hot with chutney of your choice.

Analysis per serving :

Calories (Kcal) : 322.6	Total Fat (g) / % : 4.4 (12.1 %)
Carbohydrate (g) : 61.4	Saturated Fat (g) : 0.7
Dietary Fiber (g) : 7	Monounsaturated Fat (g) : 1.7
Protein (g) : 10.2	Polyunsaturated Fat (g) : 0.9
Sodium (mg) : 139	Cholesterol (mg) : 2

Home-made Garam Masala

½ cup coriander seeds
¼ cup cumin seeds
1 tbs. black peppercorn
3 whole cinnamon sticks, each 3-inches long
2 tbs. black cloves
6 whole cardamoms
4 bay leaves, crushed

- Heat a large nonstick skillet on medium heat, until hot.
- First, dry toast the coriander seeds for 5-8 minutes or until the coriander seeds release their aroma.
- Next, toast the cumin seeds in similar manner - for 5 minutes.
- Finally, dry toast the whole black pepper, cinnamon sticks, black cloves and cardamom for 4-5 minutes. Combine the toasted spices with bay leaves and nutmeg.
- Set aside for 10 minutes to cool. Using a clean coffee mill or blender, dry grind them to a fine powder. Bottle immediately to preserve the aroma of the spices.
- Store the bottled garam masala in the freezer and use as a flavoring with your favorite vegetable or rice recipe in the place of store bought Garam masala.

Szechwan Rice   Serves : 6

This is a fragrant and extremely colorful recipe. Don't be surprised if you find this dish so irresistible that you keep sampling even before it gets to the table. Kids love making this recipe because it is so easy. Goes well with the Manchurian Soup.

1 cup raw Jasmine (fragrant) rice, **cooked in 2 cups water & cooled**
1 tbs. canola oil
¼ tsp. sesame seed oil, **optional**
½ cup finely diced onions
2 tsp. grated ginger
2 tsp. crushed garlic
1 cup each finely diced carrots **and** cabbage, **steamed**
1 cup canned corn kernels, **rinsed and drained**
1 cup frozen green peas
2 tbs. light soy sauce
1 medium green pepper, diced fine
1 cup **each** finely diced green pepper, red pepper **and** celery
½ cup finely chopped green onions
salt **and** freshly ground black pepper, to taste

- Transfer cooked rice to a large casserole. Fluff and set to cool.
- Heat the oil in a large skillet over medium-high heat and sauté the onions (with a pinch of salt) until golden brown. Add the ginger and garlic and sauté for 5 seconds. Add the steamed carrots and cabbage, canned corn kernels, and frozen green peas. Cook covered for 5 minutes.
- Add green pepper, red pepper, celery, cooked rice, green onions and soy sauce. Adjust salt and pepper to taste. Mix thoroughly until well combined and heated right through, about 10 minutes. Serve hot.

Analysis per serving :
Calories (Kcal) : 208.5
Carbohydrate (g) : 40.7
Dietary Fiber (g) : 4.1
Protein (g) : 5.6
Sodium (mg) : 316

Total Fat (g) / % : 3.2 / 13.3 %
Saturated Fat (g) : 0.3
Monounsaturated Fat (g) : 1.6
Polyunsaturated Fat (g) : 1
Cholesterol (mg) : 0

Vegetarian Paella   Serves : 6

Never been a great fan of artichokes and never will be. My love for this Spanish rice dish motivated me to alter the original recipe ever so slightly by substituting steamed asparagus for artichokes. Everything else remains the same.

2 tbs. olive oil
1 cup finely chopped leeks or onions
3 garlic cloves, crushed
¾ tsp. each thyme, basil, oregano or to taste
½ tsp. crushed red pepper or to taste
4 bay leaves
6 -8 strands of saffron
2 cups sliced mushrooms
2 cups long grain rice or converted rice
¾ - 1 tsp. salt, or to taste
4 ½ cups water
2 cups diced red or green peppers
2 cups frozen green peas
1 cup canned artichoke hearts, drained **or** 1 cup steamed asparagus

- Preheat oven to 400°F.
- Heat the oil in a large saucepan over medium-high heat. Add leeks or onions and sauté until translucent. Add garlic and sauté for 5 seconds. Add all the spices, **from thyme to saffron** and stir for 10 seconds.
- Add mushrooms and rice. Stir until well combined.
- Transfer to an ovenproof casserole. Add water and salt. Stir. **Cover** and bake in a preheated oven for 30 - 35 minutes or until rice feels cooked. Fold in the green peas, green or red peppers and artichokes or asparagus.
- Bake **uncovered,** for another 10 minutes.
- Serve hot, surrounded by lemon wedges.

```
Analysis per serving :
Calories (Kcal) : 277.1           Total Fat (g) / % : 5.0 / 15.9 %
Carbohydrate (g) : 54.7           Saturated Fat (g) : 0.4
Dietary Fiber (g) : 5.3           Monounsaturated Fat (g) : 2.7
Protein (g) : 4.7                 Polyunsaturated Fat (g) : 1.6
Sodium (mg) : 452                 Cholesterol (mg) : 0
```

Vegetable

Ecstasies

Ratatouille

Serves : 6

The first time I tasted ratatouille was in a San José restaurant. It was so good that I had to ask the restaurant manager what was in it. He said that it was a house secret and that if I guessed the ingredients right, my dinner would be on the house. Just a couple of spoons is all that it took me to figure it out, and sure enough I got my free meal, that night. I have managed to recreate the same delicious recipe for you and here it is.

1 tsp. olive oil
½ cup red onions, quartered
3 garlic cloves, crushed
¼ tsp. **each** paprika **and** ground black pepper, or to taste
4 large bay leaves
¾ tsp. **each** oregano, basil **and** thyme, or to taste
1 small eggplant, diced into 1-inch cubes
2 cups butternut squash, with skin, diced into 1-inch chunks
2 zucchinis, diced into 1-inch cubes
4 large tomatoes, diced large
2 tsp. brown sugar or sweetener of your choice
1 red pepper, diced into 1-inch pieces
1 green pepper, diced into 1-inch pieces
½ tsp. salt, or to taste

- Preheat oven to 400°F.
- Heat the oil in a large skillet over medium-high heat and sauté the onions (with a pinch of salt) until golden brown. Add garlic and the remaining spices and sauté for 5 seconds. Transfer this mixture to a large ovenproof casserole. Add the cut vegetables **(except green and red peppers)** and brown sugar.
- Cover and bake for 35-40 minutes or until vegetables are cooked. Add salt and the **green and red peppers**. Stir. Adjust seasoning to taste. Serve hot or cold with pita, steamed rice or cooked pasta.

Analysis per serving :

Calories (Kcal) : 80	Total Fat (g) / % : 1.3 (12.9 %)
Carbohydrate (g) : 17.3	Saturated Fat (g) : 0.2
Dietary Fiber (g) : 4	Monounsaturated Fat (g) : 0.6
Protein (g) : 2.8	Polyunsaturated Fat (g) : 0.3
Sodium (mg) : 63	Cholesterol (mg) : 0

Mathan Patchadi (Pumpkin or Squash Curry)
Serves : 6

Know what I like about this East-Indian recipe ? The combination of yellow pumpkin and spices. I eat this with steamed rice and a few chips on the side. I fancy this dish as it goes well with my very favorite Upma (Cream of Wheat Pilaf). Please do try it and see if you agree with me.

2 cups water, more if required
1- 2 tbs. tamarind paste, depending on how sour you like it
1 tsp. butter + 1 tsp. canola oil
2 tsp. mustard seeds
½ tsp. fenugreek seeds
¼ tsp. **asafetida powder** * *(see page 50 for information)
½ tsp.ground turmeric
½ tsp. chili powder. or to taste
4 cups, ¾-inch chunks yellow pumpkin or butternut squash
1 red **or** green pepper, diced large
2 medium tomatoes, diced large
1 - 2 tbs. brown sugar
salt, to taste

Grind to a fine paste (using a blender)
a 2-inch piece fresh coconut, cut into very fine pieces
about ¼ cup of water for grinding it to a paste,
2 tsp. black mustard seeds
2 - 3 dry red chilies
2 tbs. rice powder or cornstarch

Garnish: ¼ cup finely chopped coriander leaves

- Mix the tamarind paste in 3 cups water. Set aside.
- Heat a deep saucepan over medium-high heat. Add the butter and oil. When the butter melts, add the mustard seeds and fenugreek seeds. When they start spluttering, lower the heat. Add the asafetida, turmeric, and chili powder and sauté for 5 seconds.
- Add the prepared tamarind water, pumpkin, tomatoes, brown sugar and salt. Bring to a boil. Cook covered, on medium heat, until vegetables are soft to the touch, about 15 minutes.

- Add the green or red pepper and the ground coconut mixture. Mix thoroughly.
- When it comes to a boil, take the saucepan off the heat. This curry is a fairly thick one.
- Garnish with freshly chopped coriander leaves. Serve hot with steamed Basmati rice or bread of your choice.

Analysis per serving:
Calories (Kcal) : 107.7
Carbohydrate (g) : 20.9
Dietary Fiber (g) : 3.5
Protein (g) : 2
Sodium (mg) : 12

Total Fat (g) / % : 3 / 22.5 %
Saturated Fat (g) : 1.3
Monounsaturated Fat (g) : 0.9
Polyunsaturated Fat (g) : 0.5
Cholesterol (mg) : 1

Variation: Other Patchadis.

Here are a few suggestions to vary the vegetables in the Patchadi

You can try the following variations. (All other ingredients , vegetables and the procedure remain the same for the Patchadi recipe) :

- ♥ Okra Patchadi : 4 cups Okra - diced into 1-inch pieces.
- ♥ Eggplant Patchadi - 4 cups eggplant - diced into 1-inch cubes.
- ♥ Mango Patchadi : 4 cups semi-ripe mangoes - 1-inch chunks
- ♥ Add 1/2 cup freshly diced pineapple to original recipe.

Alu Gobi (Potato & Cauliflower Curry)   Serves : 6

This much sought after East-Indian recipe delights even the novice cook. If you want to be authentic, get your hands on Nan, a traditional East-Indian bread, that is easily available in some supermarkets as well in your local Asian food shop.

2 cups cauliflower, cut into large florets
3 large potatoes, halved and quartered (into 8 pieces)
2 tbs. canola oil
2 tsp. cumin seeds
1 cup finely diced onions
2 tsp. **each** grated ginger **and** crushed garlic
1 tbs. **each** coriander powder **and** cumin powder
½ tsp. chili powder, or to taste
1 tbs. brown sugar or sweetener of your choice
2 cups diced tomatoes
4 tbs.finely chopped coriander leaves

- Cook potatoes, until soft to the touch, in a large pot of water. Remove the potatoes and set aside. Using the same water, blanch the cauliflower (about 5 minutes). Drain and set aside.
- Heat the oil in a large nonstick skillet over medium-high heat and sauté the cumin seeds and onions (with a pinch of salt) until golden brown. Add ginger, garlic, the remaining spices and sugar and sauté for 10 seconds. Add the tomatoes and cook until the juice has evaporated.
- Add the blanched cauliflower and cooked potatoes to the tomato mixture and gently stir them in, ensuring the vegetables are completely covered with the onion/tomato mixture.
- Cook for 5 minutes or until heated through. Garnish with fresh cut coriander just before serving.
- Serve hot with steamed rice or bread of your choice.

Analysis per serving:

Calories (Kcal) : 122.3	Total Fat (g) / % : 5.1 / 35.1 %
Carbohydrate (g) : 18.3	Saturated Fat (g) : 0.4
Dietary Fiber (g) : 3.1	Monounsaturated Fat (g) : 2.7
Protein (g) : 2.8	Polyunsaturated Fat (g) : 1.5
Sodium (mg) : 127	Cholesterol (mg) : 0

Bhaingan Bhartha   Serves : 6

Yet another frequently requested East-Indian recipe. I guess it is the burnt taste of the eggplant that drives people mad with desire for this recipe. This is the only way I like my eggplant. Freezes well and tastes fresh when it is reheated.

1 large eggplant
1 to 2 tbs. canola oil
1 cup finely diced onions
2 tsp. **each** grated ginger **and** crushed garlic
2 tsp. **each** ground coriander **and** ground cumin
½ tsp. chili powder, or to taste
1 tsp. garam masala
2 tsp. brown sugar
4 cups finely chopped tomatoes
1 tbs. lemon juice
¾ tsp. salt, or to taste
3 tbs. finely chopped fresh coriander

- Slit the eggplant in half lengthwise, starting from the stem. Pierce the flesh side of the eggplant all over with a fork. Broil the eggplant, flesh side down on a greased baking sheet, until the skin is completely burnt and the fleshy portion feels soft to the touch. When cool enough, scoop out the flesh of the eggplant. Set aside in a bowl.
- Heat the oil in a large nonstick skillet over medium heat and sauté the onions (with a pinch of salt) until golden brown. Add the ginger and garlic and remaining spices and sauté for 10 seconds.
- Add the remaining ingredients. Cover and cook on low heat until liquid evaporates and it becomes a puree. It is thick enough to serve as a dip with pita or serve as a side dish with rice or bread. Serve hot or cold.

Analysis per serving :	
Calories (Kcal) : 104	Total Fat (g) / % : 5.2 / 41.1 %
Carbohydrate (g) : 14.4	Saturated Fat (g) : 0.4
Dietary Fiber (g) : 4.1	Monounsaturated Fat (g) : 2.8
Protein (g) : 2.4	Polyunsaturated Fat (g) : 1.6
Sodium (mg) : 480	Cholesterol (mg) : 0

Eggplant & Potato Moussaka   Serves: 6

Eggplant is not high in the list of vegetables I adore. However, after a lot of experimentation, I came up with my own easy-to-make, low-fat, spicy version which I do enjoy as do others who have tasted it. Hope you like it too.

1 medium eggplant, cut into ¼-inch slices
vegetable cooking spray to coat the eggplant lightly while cooking
2 medium potatoes with skin, sliced lengthwise, ½-inch thick

1 tsp. canola oil
½ cup finely chopped onion
3 cloves garlic, crushed
1 tbs. Italian seasoning or 1 tsp.**each** oregano, basil, thyme
½ tsp. chili powder, or to taste
1 cup canned crushed tomatoes
2 cups fresh, chopped tomatoes
1 tbs. brown sugar
¾ tsp. salt or to taste

Topping: ½ cup soft or Silken Tofu
            1 cup 1% cottage cheese
            ¼ cup low-fat mozzarella cheese (7%)

For the layering :   1 cup fresh bread crumbs

For the final topping : 3 tbs. grated parmesan cheese

- Preheat oven to 400°F.
- Heat a large, lightly greased, nonstick skillet over medium-high heat. Cover the skillet with a single layer of sliced eggplant. Cook until golden brown on both sides. Cook all the eggplant slices in a similar way. Spray a little oil on the eggplant slices to help speed the cooking process. Transfer the cooked eggplant to a dish or plate.
- Using the same skillet, heat the oil over medium-high heat and sauté onions (with a pinch of salt) and until golden brown. Add the crushed garlic and the remaining spices and sauté for 5 seconds. Add crushed tomatoes, fresh tomatoes, brown sugar and salt. Stir thoroughly. Bring to a boil. Remove from heat and set aside.

- Combine topping mixture in a medium sized bowl. Set aside.
- Grease a 9x13-inch ovenproof casserole.
- Layer the moussaka as follows:
  Spread ½ the tomato mixture.
  Place the potato slices in a single overlapping layer
  Spread ½ the bread crumbs
  Spread ½ the topping mixture
  Place the eggplant slices in a single overlapping layer
  Spread the remaining tomato mixture
  Spread the other ½ of the cheese mixture
  Spread the remaining bread crumbs
  Finally, top with grated parmesan cheese
- Bake for 35-40 minutes, **uncovered**, or until golden brown spots are seen on the top of the moussaka. Let stand for 10 minutes, then cut into squares to serve. Goes very well with cooked pasta or steamed rice.

Analysis per serving:
Calories (Kcal) : 175.1   Total Fat (g) / % : 4.4 / 21.4 %
Carbohydrate (g) : 24.3   Saturated Fat (g) : 1.5
Dietary Fiber (g) : 4.3   Monounsaturated Fat (g) : 1.4
Protein (g) : 11.7   Polyunsaturated Fat (g) : 1
Sodium (mg) : 667   Cholesterol (mg) : 6

Dynamite Vegetable Chili   Serves : 6

This chili will fool the most dedicated meat eater. TVP chunks do the trick. While perfecting this chili, I found that a mix of the right spices helped bring out the authentic flavor of Mexico, the way it was meant to be.

1 cup dry TVP nuggets, **soaked in hot water for ½ hour**
1 tsp. canola oil
1 cup finely chopped onion
3 cloves garlic, crushed
1 tsp. **each** coriander powder **and** oregano
½ tsp. **each** cumin powder **and** chili powder
1 cup **each** diced carrots **and** diced turnip
2 cups canned, crushed tomatoes + 2 cups water
1 tbs. brown sugar or sweetener of your choice
¾ tsp. salt, or to taste
1 cup **each** diced celery **and** red or green pepper
2 cups **canned or cooked** red kidney beans, **rinsed and drained**
½ cup water, if required
1 tsp. unsweetened cocoa

Garnish: ½ cup freshly chopped coriander leaves

- Drain soaked TVP chunks. Using a food processor or blender break up the TVP chunks to a fine mince. Set aside.
- Heat the oil in a large, deep saucepan over medium-high heat and sauté onions (with a pinch of salt) until golden brown. Add the crushed garlic and the remaining spices and sauté for 10 seconds.
- Add the minced TVP, carrots, turnip, crushed tomatoes, water and brown sugar. Mix thoroughly. Bring it to a boil. Cover, reduce heat to medium, and cook for 20 minutes or until the vegetables are cooked (do not overcook the vegetables).
- Finally, add the salt, celery, red or green pepper, the cooked beans, more water if required, and cocoa. Stir. Cook for another 10 minutes until the chili is well combined. Adjust seasoning to taste.
- Serve garnished with chopped coriander leaves.

Analysis per serving:
Calories (Kcal) : 150.3
Carbohydrate (g) : 28.5
Dietary Fiber (g) : 9.7
Protein (g) : 9.8
Sodium (mg) : 561

Total Fat (g) / % : 1.5 / 8.1 %
Saturated Fat (g) : 0.2
Monounsaturated Fat (g) : 0.6
Polyunsaturated Fat (g) : 0.4
Cholesterol (mg) : 0

TVP (Textured Vegetable Protein)

The versatility of the TVP abounds and the things that you can create with this high protein, low fat ingredient are truly amazing.

- TVP is made from defatted soy flour (soya bean flour with the fat removed from it).
- TVP has a tan color and comes in a variety of shapes.
- It is available in some grocery stores, but will definitely be found in your local health food stores.

TVP comes in different shapes:

- small bits that resemble gravel
- medium sized ones that look like pebbles
- medium sized flat ones that look like mini patties
- large ones that look like dry dog food.

I would like to share with you an anecdote concerning TVP:

I like storing my pasta and beans in tall translucent, glass bottles. One of these bottles contained my large TVP. One of my cooking school students saw this bottle of TVP. As she had never seen TVP and did not know what it was, what she blurted out made me chuckle for a few days. She said " Boy, for someone who doesn't have a dog, you certainly have a lot of dog biscuits around". It took me only a few seconds to realize what she was talking about !.

Mattar Paneer (Peas and Cottage Cheese Curry))
Serves : 6

My husband's absolute #1 favorite East-Indian delicacy. It will caress your taste buds and give you sweet dreams. I have made it ultra low-fat so that you can savor it guilt-free.

vegetable cooking spray to sauté Paneer
2 cups ½-inch cubed Paneer (page 110)

1 tbs. canola oil
1 cup finely chopped onions
2 tsp. **each** grated ginger **and** crushed garlic
½ tsp. turmeric
½ tsp. chili powder, or to taste
1 tbs. garam masala (see page: 114)
1 tbs. brown sugar or sweetener of your choice
2 cups canned crushed tomatoes
1 tbs. tomato paste
2 cups frozen green peas
1 cup hot water or more, if required

Garnish: 3 tbs. chopped coriander leaves

- Heat a medium sized fry pan or nonstick skillet on medium-high and spray a little cooking spray to coat the bottom of the skillet. Add the diced paneer and stir to coat all over. Cook all sides of the cubed paneer to a golden brown color. Set aside.
- Heat the oil in a large non-stick skillet on medium-high heat. and sauté onions (with a pinch of salt) until golden brown. Add the ginger, garlic, the remaining dry spices, brown sugar and sauté for 5 seconds. Add the crushed tomatoes and tomato paste. Stir to combine. Cover. Cook for 20 minutes or until the juice from the tomatoes has been reduced considerably.
- Add the frozen green peas. Stir to combine. Add the water, prepared paneer and salt. Cover and cook until peas are soft, but not overcooked (about 12 minutes).
- Serve hot, garnished with chopped coriander leaves.
- Serve with steamed rice or bread of your choice.

```
Analysis per serving:
Calories (Kcal) : 230.2          Total Fat (g) / % : 13.3 /51.1 %
Carbohydrate (g) : 15.9          Saturated Fat (g) : 7
Dietary Fiber (g) : 4.2          Monounsaturated Fat (g) : 4.4
Protein (g) : 12.9               Polyunsaturated Fat (g) : 1.2
Sodium (mg) : 235                Cholesterol (mg) : 41
```

Paneer Fact Sheet

Paneer is an east-indian, home-made cottage cheese that is used in numerous East-Indian recipes. It can be made at home but I prefer to buy the store bought variety to ease my life a wee bit !! It is available at most East-Indian grocery stores.

Useful information you could use about Paneer:

- Paneer is not North American cottage cheese .
- There are low-fat versions of Paneer .
- Paneer does not melt .
- Paneer retains its shape when cooked..
- I sauté the whole slab of Paneer on a a lightly greased skillet to a deep golden brown. When cool to touch, I cut up the slab into small cubes and keep them handy in the freezer to use in any vegetable recipe or as an add - on for a vegetable Pilaf.
- A few pieces in any rice pilaf or vegetable curry greatly enhances the flavor giving it a rich taste.
- You can freeze the cubed Paneer and use it as and when you require it.

Sicilian Bean Casserole   Serves: 6

This hearty, nutritious bean casserole owes its rich, buttery taste to the lima beans. This recipe develops more flavor if made a day ahead (perfect for the working person). Simple, yet elegant, this delicious recipe looks and feels like a masterpiece, even when made by a novice.

2 tsp. canola oil
1 cup finely chopped onions
1 tbs. crushed garlic
2 tsp. dried Italian seasoning
1/4 tsp. crushed red pepper, or to taste
1/4 tsp. ground pepper, or to taste
4 bay leaves
1 cup sliced carrots, 3/4-inch piece chunks.
1 cup sliced celery, 3/4-inch piece chunks
2 large potatoes, cut into big chunks (halved and quartered)
1 large yam, cut into big chunks
4 tbs. flour mixed in 3 cups of lukewarm water, no lumps
3/4 - 1 tsp. salt, or to taste
2 cups **cooked or canned** large lima beans (a.k.a butter beans),
                                         (rinsed & drained)
1 cup green or red pepper, cut into big chunks

- Preheat oven to 400°F.
- Heat the oil in a large skillet over medium-high heat and sauté onions (with a pinch of salt) until golden brown. Add garlic and all the spices and sauté for 10 seconds.
- Transfer the prepared onion mixture to a large ovenproof casserole. Add the carrots, celery, potatoes, yams and the flour/water mixture. **Cover and cook** for 30 minutes. **Remove cover**. Add the cooked beans, red or green pepper and salt. Stir thoroughly. Adjust seasoning to taste. Cook uncovered for 10 minutes.
- Goes well with steamed rice or cooked pasta.

Analysis per serving:

Calories (Kcal) : 310.3

Carbohydrate (g) : 59.6

Dietary Fiber (g) : 14.5

Protein (g) : 15.1

Sodium (mg) : 405

Total Fat (g) / % : 2.2 / 6.1 %

Saturated Fat (g) : 0.3

Monounsaturated Fat (g) : 0.9

Polyunsaturated Fat (g) : 0.8

Cholesterol (mg) : 0

Variation:
Pasta cooking Tips & Variations

To cook Pasta:

- *Bring water to a boil (use 4 times the volume of pasta).*
- *Add the pasta and cook for 8 minutes until pasta is al dente (soft, but fairly firm to the bite).*
- *Small pastas take less time to cook.*
- *Never add salt or oil when cooking pasta .*
- *Drain the cooked pasta. Transfer it to a large serving dish. Add 1 tablespoon of grated parmesan and a few drops of olive oil for every 2 cups of cooked pasta. Toss and serve with vegetable topping of your choice. Excellent with "Vegetarian Sloppy Joes" (page 115) or the Sicilian Bean Casserole (page 111).*
- *Another way to serve pasta is to add 1 tablespoon of the "Verdant Pesto" (see page 41) to every 2 cups of cooked pasta and serve steamed vegetables on the side.*

Leela's Okra Amti Dumpty   Serves : 6

y mother is an ace at making this recipe and its aroma is reminiscent of her. My heart is flooded with warm memories everytime I make this dish. Whenever I visit her I ask her to make this dish. I got this recipe from her when she came to our home in Hamilton.

½ cup raw mung dal (yellow lentils) ,cooked until soft and mushy
1 tsp. butter
1 tsp. canola oil
1 tsp. mustard seeds
1 tsp. cumin seeds
1 cup finely diced onions
½ tsp. **each** ground turmeric, asafetida & chili powder
2 tsp. Amti powder (page 114)
2 medium potatoes, diced medium
4 cups sliced Okra, ½-inch thick
2 tbs. tamarind paste
2 tbs. brown sugar
4 cups water
¾ - 1 tsp. salt, or to taste

Garnish : 1/2 cup finely chopped coriander leaves

- **Have the mung dal cooked and ready before starting this recipe**.
- Heat the butter and oil in a large nonstick saucepan or Dutchoven on medium heat. When the oil gets hot add the mustard seeds and cumin seeds. The mustard seeds will start spluttering. At that point add the onions and sauté them until translucent. Add the spices and sauté for 10 seconds.
- Add the vegetables and stir them in. Add the tamarind paste, brown sugar, salt and water. Bring the whole thing to a rolling boil. Lower the heat to medium-low. Cook until the vegetables are soft to the touch but not overcooked.
- Stir in the **cooked lentils** and bring the Amti to to a boil.
- Garnish with coriander leaves. Serve hot with steamed rice or bread of your choice.

Analysis per serving:

Calories (Kcal) : 119.9

Carbohydrate (g) : 22.3

Dietary Fiber (g) : 5.2

Protein (g) : 4.7

Sodium (mg) : 534

Total Fat (g) / % : 1.8 / 12.9%

Saturated Fat (g) : 0.6

Monounsaturated Fat (g) : 0.7

Polyunsaturated Fat (g) : 0.3

Cholesterol (mg) : 2

Homemade Amti Powder

This powder is my mother's specialty and now you can enjoy it too. I always make a double batch. Keeps fresh in the freezer (stored in airtight containers) for a few months.

1 cup Coriander seeds

¼ cup Cumin seeds

1 tbs. black peppercorn

3 whole cinnamon sticks, each 3-inches long

2 tbs. black cloves

4 whole cardamoms

- Heat a large nonstick skillet on medium heat, until hot.
- First, dry toast the coriander seeds for 5-8 minutes or until the seeds release their aroma.
- Next, toast the cumin seeds in similar manner for 5 minutes.
- Finally, dry toast the whole black pepper, cinnamon sticks, black cloves and cardamom for 4-5 minutes.
- Combine all the toasted spices and let them cool completely.
- Using a clean coffee mill or blender, dry grind them to a fine powder. Bottle immediately to preserve the aroma of the spices.
- Store the bottled Amti powder in the freezer and use as a flavoring with your favourite vegetable or rice recipe.

Jumbo Jambalaya   Serves : 6

Vegetarian Jambalaya is unheard of. Although this recipe contains no chicken or sausage, you will still enjoy the traditional Louisiana taste - the low-fat vegetarian way. I find it gets too messy when you cook the rice (the traditional way) with the other ingredients. I prefer serving the jambalaya on a bed of steamed rice.

1 tsp. canola oil
1 cup finely chopped onions
2 tbs. crushed garlic
4 bay leaves
1 tsp. **each** thyme, **and** basil
½ tsp. ground cayenne pepper
½ tsp. **each ground** nutmeg, ground cinnamon **and** ground cloves
1 cup chopped celery
3 ½ cups canned plum tomatoes, coarsely chopped
3 tbs. tomato paste
1 tsp. brown sugar or sweetener of your choice
4 cups water
1 cup **each** red pepper **and** green pepper, diced into 1-inch pieces
4 **tofu** hot dogs, cut ¾-inch pieces **(can be found in almost any supermarket**
¾ tsp. salt, or to taste
Garnish: 1 tbs. freshly chopped parsley

- Heat the oil in a large saucepan over medium-high heat and sauté onions (with a pinch of salt) until golden brown. Add the garlic and the remaining spices and sauté for 5 seconds. Add the celery, tomatoes, tomato paste and water and cook for 15 minutes.
- Add the peppers, the tofu hot dogs and salt. Adjust seasoning to taste. Cook for 10 minutes, on low heat. Garnish with chopped parsley. Serve hot, on a bed of steamed rice with a light salad.

Analysis per serving :	
Calories (Kcal) : 79.8	Total Fat (g) / % : 2.9 / 28.6 %
Carbohydrate (g) : 11.4	Saturated Fat (g) : 0.4
Dietary Fiber (g) : 3.0	Monounsaturated Fat (g) : 0.9
Protein (g) : 4.6	Polyunsaturated Fat (g) : 1.3
Sodium (mg) : 360	Cholesterol (mg) : 0

Vegetarian Sloppy Joes   Serves : 6

This recipe illustrates just what television can do for you. While channel surfing one afternoon I saw some children devouring sloppy Joe's (America's favourite food) and decided we needed a healthy vegetarian version. Takes only a few minutes to put together. Here it is.

1 tsp. canola oil
1 cup finely chopped onions
2 tbs. crushed garlic
1 tsp. **each** basil, oregano, thyme **and** paprika
3 ½ cups canned crushed tomatoes
2 tsp. brown sugar or sweetener of your choice
2 cups water
2 red peppers, seeded **and** diced 1-inch pieces
2 cups TVP bits, small variety **(see page 108 for information)**
¾ tsp. salt, or to taste

- Heat the oil in a large saucepan over medium-high heat and sauté the onions (with a pinch of salt) until golden brown. Add the garlic and the remaining spices and sauté for 10 seconds.
- Add the crushed tomatoes, brown sugar, water and the TVP. Cook covered for 20 minutes. Add the red pepper and salt. Adjust seasoning to taste.
- Serve on buns. I personally like Sloppy Joes on cooked pasta or steamed rice.

Analysis per serving :
Calories (Kcal) : 94.7
Carbohydrate (g) : 17.6
Dietary Fiber (g) : 6.2
Protein (g) : 8.9
Sodium (mg) : 380

Total Fat (g) / % : 1.3 / 10.1 %
Saturated Fat (g) : 0.1
Monounsaturated Fat (g) : 0.5
Polyunsaturated Fat (g) : 0.5
Cholesterol (mg) : 0

Muffins

(the muffins need to be
refrigerated the same day they are
baked, as they have no oil to
preserve them)

Breads

Flatbreads

&

Cakes

Hawaiian Fruit Muffins   Makes : 12 jumbo muffins

These moist, fruit-packed muffins are a light, nutritious snack. In my house, a couple of these muffins with a glass of milk, is breakfast. You can easily get 18 medium muffins out of the same recipe. I always have these on hand for a quick energy boost.

Wet Ingredients:
2 cups mashed bananas (about 3 bananas)
1 cup canned crushed pineapple with juice
2 cups finely chopped apples with skin (about 4 medium apples)
½ cup raisins, **washed and soaked** in warm water (½ hour)
2 egg-whites, well beaten
1 tbs. vanilla extract
¼ tsp. coconut extract (optional)
½ cup water, more if required

Dry ingredients:
1 cup unbleached white flour
1 cup whole-wheat flour
1 cup oatbran
4 tsp. baking powder
1 tbs. ground allspice
½ cup brown sugar or sweetener of your choice

- Preheat oven to 400°F. Lightly grease a 12 cup muffin pan.
- In a large bowl, combine the wet ingredients. Set aside.
- In another large bowl, combine the dry ingredients. Fold in wet ingredients without overmixing. The batter will be fairly moist. If the batter is too thick, add a little water. Divide mixture evenly into the prepared muffin pan
- Bake for 5 minutes. Reduce heat to 350°F and bake for another 25 minutes or until golden brown. Remove the muffins from the tin and transfer to a wire rack to cool for 5 minutes.

Analysis per muffin :

Calories (Kcal) : 199.4	Total Fat (g) / % : 1.2/ 5 %
Carbohydrate (g) : 48.2	Saturated Fat (g) : 0.3
Dietary Fiber (g) : 5	Monounsaturated Fat (g) : 0.3
Protein (g) : 4.9	Polyunsaturated Fat (g) : 0.5
Sodium (mg) : 209	Cholesterol (mg) : 0

Carr-Orange Quinoa Muffins
Makes : 12 Jumbo Muffins

Quinoa (pronounced KEEN_WA), an ancient grain, is a nutritional powerhouse. When toasted, the mild, nutty flavor blends pleasingly, with the rest of the ingredients. This fresh tasting muffin is a definite crowd pleaser. Quinoa must be rinsed, drained and toasted before using it to get rid of its bitter covering.

Wet Ingredients:
½ cup honey
4 egg-whites, well beaten
1 cup buttermilk or nonfat yogurt
1 cup frozen, unsweetened orange juice concentrate
1 cup warm water to thin the orange juice concentrate
½ cup raisins
2 cups grated carrots
2 tbs. grated orange peel
1 tsp. vanilla extract

Dry Ingredients:
½ cup Quinoa, **must be rinsed clean and set aside to drain** (½ hour)
2 cups unbleached white flour
¾ cup cream of wheat
4 tbs. baking powder
1 tsp. baking soda
¼ tsp. salt, or to taste
3 tbs. black poppy seeds

- In a medium saucepan, dry toast quinoa, on medium-high heat, for 15 minutes, and on high heat for 5 minutes. The quinoa turns golden color and will emit a nutty aroma. Set aside to cool.
- Preheat the oven to 400°F. Lightly grease a muffin pan.
- In a large bowl, combine the wet ingredients.
- In another large bowl, combine the dry ingredients. Add wet ingredients, all at once, to the dry ingredients and stir until well combined. Take care not to overmix. Divide mixture evenly into the prepared muffin pan.

119

- Bake for 5 minutes. Reduce heat to 375°F and bake for another 25 minutes or until golden brown. Remove the muffins from the tin and transfer to a wire rack to cool for 10 minutes.

Analysis per muffin :	
Calories (Kcal) : 279.1	Total Fat (g) / % : 1.9 / 6 %
Carbohydrate (g) : 59.8	Saturated Fat (g) : 0.2
Dietary Fiber (g) : 2.5	Monounsaturated Fat (g) : 0.3
Protein (g) : 7.9	Polyunsaturated Fat (g) : 1
Sodium (mg) : 557	Cholesterol (mg) : 0.

Important notes on Muffins :

♥ All my muffins **must** be refrigerated, on the same day they are baked, in an airtight container or plastic bags with seal.

♥ They keep fresh for a week, when refrigerated.

♥ Freezes well. Refrigerated or frozen muffins have to be brought to room temperature before you consume them.

♥ Heat them in a microwave oven on high for 25 seconds before serving.

Time saving tips to make muffins:
(You won't believe how much time you'll be saving)

♥ The wet Ingredients : Make a double batch of the fruit that the recipe calls for minus the egg-whites and freeze one half. A day before you are going to bake, take the frozen fruit mixture out of the freezer and leave in the refrigerator section to defrost. Incorporate the egg-whites, as per recipe instructions, the day you make the muffins.

♥ The dry ingredients: Make a double batch of the dry ingredients minus the baking powdered and baking soda. and put away one half in an airtight container. Incorporate baking powder and baking soda, according to recipe instructions, the day you make the muffins.

♥ I beat up the unused egg yolks with a cup of water, and use it as a natural fertilizer , to water my outdoor plants (that may account for the huge Purple Clematis that bloomed this summer - another reason being , I don't have to worry about my clematis suffering from high cholesterol).

Mexicasa Corn Muffins
Makes : 12 large muffins

The aroma from these muffins is intoxicating. This versatile muffin is good on its own for breakfast or as an accompaniment to my vegetarian chili or even great when served with a light salad.

Wet Ingredients
4 egg whites, well beaten
2 cups buttermilk or nonfat yogurt
½ to 1 cup low-fat, shredded cheddar cheese

Dry Ingredients:
1 ½ cups unbleached white flour
1 ½ cups yellow cornmeal
1 tbs. baking powder
1 tsp. baking soda
4 tbs. sugar or sweetener of your choice
1/8 tsp. salt

- Preheat oven to 400°F. Lightly grease muffin pan.
- In a large bowl, combine the wet ingredients.
- In a separate bowl, combine the dry ingredients. Add the wet mixture, all at once, to the dry mixture. Mix until well combined.
- Divide mixture evenly into the prepared muffin pan.
- Bake for 5 minutes. Reduce heat to 375°F and bake for another 12 minutes or until golden brown. Remove the muffins from the tin and transfer to a wire rack to cool for 5 minutes.

Analysis per muffin :

Calories (Kcal) : 176.1	Total Fat (g) / % : 0.8 / 4.5%
Carbohydrate (g) : 32.9	Saturated Fat (g) : 0.3
Dietary Fiber (g) : 1.3	Monounsaturated Fat (g) : 0.2
Protein (g) : 7.6	Polyunsaturated Fat (g) : 0.2
Sodium (mg) : 361	Cholesterol (mg) : 2

Sheera (Eggless Cake)   Serves : 10

This Indian dessert / sweetmeat (all cake desserts in India are called sweetmeats-no relation to meat, whatsoever) is a sheer delight. This recipe is a boon to all novices who will feel as if they have accomplished an arduous task. You can keep this as a standby recipe when unexpected guests drop in and you are rushed for time.

Wet Ingredients:
½ cup sugar
2 tbs. melted butter
1 cup nonfat yogurt
1 cup skimmed milk
1 tsp. ground cardamom
½ cup raisins

Dry Ingredients :
2 cups cream of wheat
1 tbs. baking powder
2 tbs. toasted, broken cashews

- Preheat oven at 350°F. Lightly grease a 9-inch nonstick cake pan.
- In a medium sized bowl, combine the wet ingredients. Set aside.
- In a large bowl, combine the dry ingredients. Gently whisk in the wet ingredients, ensuring there are no lumps.
- Pour batter into the prepared pan. Bake for 35 - 40 minutes or until golden brown.
- Remove the sheera from the cake pan and transfer to a wire rack to cool for 5 minutes. Cut into desired shape and serve warm at room temperature.

Analysis per serving:
Calories (Kcal) : 239.8
Carbohydrate (g) : 45.9
Dietary Fiber (g) : 1.7
Protein (g) : 6.3
Sodium (mg) :166

Total Fat (g) / % : 3.7 / 13.7 %
Saturated Fat (g) : 1.6
Monounsaturated Fat (g) : 1.1
Polyunsaturated Fat (g) : 0.2
Cholesterol (mg) : 7

Biscotti with Nuts   makes : 45 cookies

I don't know why coffee shops charge so much for something that is so easy and inexpensive to make. I keep these handy, especially when we travel, to dip in my favorite cappuccino. I refrigerate them in airtight containers.

Wet Ingredients:
1 egg
3 egg whites
1 tbs. vanilla extract
1 tbs. fresh lemon rind

Dry Ingredients :
2/3 cup sugar or sweetener of your choice
2 cups unbleached white flour + ½ cup flour for final kneading
2 tsp. baking soda
¼ tsp. salt
½ cup hazelnuts **or** almonds, toasted **and** crushed lightly

- Preheat oven to 325°F. Lightly grease a large cookie sheet.
- In a medium bowl, combine the wet ingredients.
- In a large bowl, combine the dry ingredients. Add wet mixture to the dry mixture, all at once, to form a fairly soft dough.
- Knead the dough for a few minutes, adding a little flour if it is too sticky. The dough, when done, will be fairly soft.
- Divide the dough into three equal portions. With floured hands form each portion into flat logs, about 10-inches long and 2-inches wide. Place the logs on the cookie sheet, 3-inches apart.
- Bake for 30-35 minutes. Remove from oven and set aside to cool for 10 minutes.
- Meanwhile, reduce heat to 250°F.
- Cut the lightly cooled, baked logs at an angle into ¾-inch thick segments. Arrange them on the cookie sheet and bake 10-12 minutes on each side.
- **Turn the oven to off position**. Leave the Biscotti **in the oven for 15-20 minutes to crisp further**.
- Remove the Biscotti from oven. When it cools down, store in airtight containers. and enjoy it.

```
Analysis per Biscotti :
Calories (Kcal) : 49.1          Total Fat (g) / % : 1 / 18.3 %
Carbohydrate (g) : 8.7          Saturated Fat (g) : 0.1
Dietary Fiber (g) : 0.2         Monounsaturated Fat (g) : 0.6
Protein (g) : 1.4              Polyunsaturated Fat (g) : 0.2
Sodium (mg) : 73               Cholesterol (mg) : 5
```

Variation for Biscotti

Lemon Poppyseed Biscotti :
Eliminate the vanilla extract and nuts and add the following -
1 tbs. lemon rind , 1/2 cup frozen lemon concentrate, 3 tbs. black
poppy seeds, and 1/2 cup flour or more, if needed

Three-Ginger Biscotti :
Eliminate the nuts and add the following - 2 tsp. ground ginger,
3 tbs. minced crystallized ginger and 1 tbs. grated fresh ginger.

Chocolate Chip Biscotti (definitely not low-fat) :
Eliminate the nuts and add 1/2 cup chocolate chips

Chuckie's Cornmeal Bread
Makes: 1 loaf   (Serves : 8)

This irresistible bread does not go beyond a single sitting, especially with my husband who can't wait to get his hands on it even before the poor bread can cool. This bread is so good, it will turn anyone into a glutton. Excellent with the vegetarian chili or any of the soups, even the hot and sour soup.

¼ cup cornmeal + ½ cup boiling water to cook the cornmeal

To proof yeast: ½ cup warm water(110^0F)
1 tbs. brown sugar
1 tbs. dry active yeast

1/8 cup water
2-½ cups unbleached white flour
½ cup instant skimmed milk powder
¾ tsp. salt, or to taste
2 tsp. canola oil., **for kneading**
a little canola oil to grease the bowl

- In a deep saucepan, bring half a cup of water to a boil. Add the cornmeal in a single stream stirring it in with a whisk to prevent lumping. When all the water has been absorbed transfer the cooked cornmeal to a platter. Set aside to cool.
- **Meanwhile proof the yeast as follows:** Combine ½ cup of the warm water, brown sugar and the yeast. Stir to dissolve yeast and let stand undisturbed until bubbly, for about 10 minutes.
- In a large bowl, combine the proofed yeast, cooked and cooled cornmeal, and the remaining ingredients, **except oil**, to form a soft pliable dough. Oil the palm of your hands and knead the dough for a few more minutes. Set aside covered, in a large greased bowl, for an hour or until dough has doubled in size.
- Punch to release air. Knead and shape into ball and place in a greased loaf pan, covered, for a further 20 minutes.
- Heat oven to 375^0F. Bake for 25 to 30 minutes or until golden. When done, the loaf should sound hollow when tapped at the bottom.
- Serve warm with chili or a warm soup.

Analysis per serving :
Calories (Kcal) : 203.9
Carbohydrate (g) : 38.7
Dietary Fiber (g) : 0.7
Protein (g) : 7.7
Sodium (mg) : 242

Total Fat (g) / % : 1.7 / 7.7 %
Saturated Fat (g) : 0.2
Monounsaturated Fat (g) : 0.8
Polyunsaturated Fat (g) : 0.5
Cholesterol (mg) : 1

Challah (Egg Bread)   Serves : 8

The Challah mavens in our family, my husband and his cousins, are delighted every time I bake challah. When Pearl, my mother-in-law, tasted my version for the first time, she said it looked and tasted just like what her mother used to make. Guess it brought back a lot of memories !! Everytime I make challah, I love to see the expression of rapture it brings to my Chuck's (hubby's) face.

To proof the yeast:

> ½ cup lukewarm water (110°F)
> 1 tbs. active dry yeast
> 1 tsp. sugar

1 tbs. honey
1 large egg + 1 yolk, beaten (**set aside 2 tbs. beaten egg for egg wash**)
½ tsp. salt
½ cup low-fat grated cheddar cheese (optional)
2 cups unbleached white flour + 1/2 cup flour, for kneading
2 tsp. oil, for final kneading

For topping : 2 tsp. sesame seeds (optional)

- In a small bowl, mix the yeast and sugar in ½ cup lukewarm water. Stir. Let the mixture rest for 10 minutes or until foamy.
- In a large bowl, combine the honey, beaten eggs, salt, cheddar cheese, and the proofed yeast. Stir thoroughly until well combined.
- Add the flour, gradually, to make a smooth but fairly stiff dough, about 12 minutes.
- Oil the palm of your hands to work the dough and coat with the oil.
- Transfer to a greased bowl. Cover with a damp cloth and set aside to rise in a warm draft free place, until doubled in volume, about 1 hour.
- Divide the dough into 3 equal parts. Using your fingers and the palm of your hand, roll the dough, one part at a time to form a smooth log about 12-inches long. You should have 3 logs.
- Braid the three logs fairly tightly and tuck each end in to give it a neat appearance. Carefully transfer the braided dough to an oiled baking sheet. Cover with a damp cloth and let rise about another 1 hour or until nearly doubled in volume.

- Preheat oven to 350°F. Brush the braided dough with the reserved 2 tbs. beaten egg. Sprinkle the top with sesame seeds. Bake for 25 minutes or to the point where the bread begins to turn a light golden color.
- Reduce oven temperature to 325°F. Bake for 20 minutes. Test if done, by tapping the bottom of the bread which should sound hollow. Cool for 10 minutes, before serving.

```
Analysis per serving  (with cheddar cheese) :
Calories (Kcal) : 149.5 (168.5)      Total Fat (g) / % : 2 / 12.2 % (2.5 / 14.1 %)
Carbohydrate (g) : 27.3 (27.5)       Saturated Fat (g) :  0.4 (0.7)
Dietary Fiber (g) : 0.4 (0.4)        Monounsaturated Fat (g) : 0.8 (1)
Protein (g) : 5.3 (7)                Polyunsaturated Fat (g) : 0.6 (0.6)
Sodium (mg) : 216 (259)              Cholesterol (mg) : 27 (28)
```

Challah Variation

- Substitute raisins for cheese.
- Omit both cheese and raisins for a plain challah.

Other shapes to try:
- After the 1st rise, divide the dough into 8 small portions and make a tight ball with each one. Set them in the shape of a flower, in a round pan, for the second rise. Bake as per instructions for the challah.
- After the 1st rise, roll the dough into a long rope about 18-inches long. Coil it around like a snake and set it in a round pan, for a second rise. Bake as per instructions for the challah.

Grilled Vegetable Flatbread   Makes : 6

Served warm with Velvety Vanilla Yogurt Dip (page 40), this filling flatbread explodes with fresh seasonal vegetables making it a one-dish meal. It converts easily into an appetizer if you cut it up into bite-size portions. I love it just as it comes out of the oven.

For the dough:

1 tbs. active dry yeast
1 tsp. sugar
¼ cup warm water (105°F - 115°F)
2 cups whole-wheat flour with bran
1 cup unbleached white flour
¾ cup warm skim milk, or more if required
salt and cracked pepper, to taste
1 tsp. olive oil, **for final kneading only**

For the filling:

2 tsp. olive oil
½ cup finely diced onion
½ - 1 tsp. **each** dry oregano **and** thyme
½ cup finely diced potatoes, steamed until soft
½ cup finely broken broccoli, steamed until soft
½ cup **each** finely diced celery **and** carrots, steamed until soft
½ cup finely diced red peppers
½ tsp. each salt and ground pepper, or to taste
2 tbs. chopped fresh parsley

To prepare the dough

- In a small bowl, combine yeast , ¼ cup warm water and sugar. Stir. Set aside for 10 minutes or until frothy.
- Meanwhile, in a large bowl, **except the olive oil**, combine the prepared yeast with the remaining dough ingredients to make a fairly soft dough. Oil your palm with a teaspoon of olive oil and knead to cover the dough all over with the oil. Cover and set aside for an hour.

To prepare the vegetable stuffing:

- Heat oil in a large nonstick skillet on medium-high heat and sauté onions (with a pinch of salt) until golden brown. Add the oregano and thyme and sauté for 5 seconds. Add the steamed vegetables, salt and pepper. Toss well to combine. Adjust seasoning to taste. Cook until all the water has been absorbed. Stir in the parsley. When cool enough to handle, divide the prepared vegetables into 6 equal portions and make a ball with each portion. Set aside.

To shape the Bread:

- Lightly grease 2 large baking sheets. Set aside.
- Divide the prepared dough into 6 equal portions. Shape each one into a round ball and keep all of them covered in a large bowl.
- Take one ball of dough and roll it flat, with a rolling pin, into an 8-inch round. Place one portion of the prepared "vegetable filling" in the centre of the rolled out dough.
- **Pull the outer edges of the rolled out dough to enclose the "vegetable filling" completely (The end result should look like a tennis ball with vegetable filling).**
- Flatten it gently applying very little pressure with a rolling pin to form a 6-inch circle. Transfer it to the prepared baking sheet.
- Finish the remaining dough and vegetable filling in a similar manner.
- Brush prepared flatbread with olive oil. Set aside for a second rise in a draft-free place for another 30 minutes.
- Set the oven to broil. Grill flattened bread on one side for 6-8 minutes or until golden. Turn them over gently with a spatula. Grill the uncooked side for 6-8 minutes, or until golden.
- Cool the grilled bread on a wire rack. Serve warm as is or with dip of your choice.

Analysis per flatbread :
Calories (Kcal) : 269.1   Total Fat (g) / % : 3.5 / 11.2 %
Carbohydrate (g) : 52   Saturated Fat (g) : 0.5
Dietary Fiber (g) : 6.6   Monounsaturated Fat (g) : 1.8
Protein (g) : 10.2   Polyunsaturated Fat (g) : 0.6
Sodium (mg) : 261   Cholesterol (mg) : 1

Any Berry Cheese Cake   Serves : 10

This is the only cheese cake I make in my house. My greatest joy was the first time my husband tried it and said he loved it. Reason being, he shuns cheesecake because of its fat and sugar content. This ultra low-fat version goes down smooth, and is wonderful with cappuccino or espresso.

Cake Crust :
1 cup **finely powdered** cornflakes **or** 10 arrowroot cookies, crushed
1 tsp. low-fat margarine for coating the cake pan

Cheese Cake Filling :
3 egg-whites + 1 whole yolk, well beaten
1 cup **low-fat**, ricotta cheese **or** pressed cottage cheese
1 ½ cup Silken Tofu
1 cup low-fat yogurt, drained for ½ hour
4 tbs. all purpose flour
¼ cup sugar or sweetener of your choice
2 tbs. fresh lemon juice
1 tbs. vanilla extract
1 tbs. fresh lemon rind (grated rind of 3/4 lemon)

Final Addition : 2 cups fresh berries **or** 2 cups frozen berries

- Preheat oven to 380°F. Grease a 10-inch springform pan with margarine. Press powdered cornflakes **or** powdered arrowroot cookies to cover the greased pan. Set aside in the refrigerator.
- Using a food processor or blender, blend all the ingredients in "cheese cake filling" to a smooth consistency. Transfer to a work bowl. Gently fold in the berries. Pour mixture into prepared cake pan.
- Bake for 1 hour or until set. Remove from oven and let chill for atleast 2 hours, before serving the cake.

Analysis per serving :

Calories (Kcal) : 137	Total Fat (g) / % : 4.5 / 28.5 %
Carbohydrate (g) : 16.1	Saturated Fat (g) : 1.7
Dietary Fiber (g) : 1.2	Monounsaturated Fat (g) : 1.4
Protein (g) : 8.2	Polyunsaturated Fat (g) : 1.1
Sodium (mg) : 96	Cholesterol (mg) : 29

Haresi

Serves: 6

The first time I became aware of this recipe, I was shocked at the amount of butter, sugar, and sugar syrup that went into it. After many attempts, I have managed to create a low-fat version without sacrificing any of the taste. Rose water and orange blossom water are the two key flavoring agents and can be found at any Middle-Eastern grocery store.

Wet ingredients:
½ cup sugar or sweetener of your choice
1 cup nonfat yogurt
2 cups skim milk
3 tbs. lemon juice
½ tsp.**each** rose water **and** orange blossom water

Dry ingredients:
2 cups cream of wheat
1 tbs. baking powder
2 tbs. toasted walnuts **or** broken pistachio nuts, optional

- Preheat oven at 350°F. Lightly grease a 10-inch springform pan.
- In a medium sized bowl, combine the wet ingredients. Set aside.
- In a large bowl, combine the dry ingredients. Gently blend in the wet ingredients ensuring that they are well combined and free of lumps. Pour prepared batter into the prepared cake pan.
- Bake for 35-40 minutes or until golden brown. To get a golden crust, you could broil the haresi in the oven for 4 to 5 minutes.
- Cut neat wedges and serve warm with frozen yogurt or serve cold as is.

Analysis per serving:	
Calories (Kcal) : 207.8	Total Fat (g) / % : 1.5 / 6.6 %
Carbohydrate (g) : 41.5	Saturated Fat (g): 0.2
Dietary Fiber (g) : 1.4	Monounsaturated Fat (g) : 0.2
Protein (g) : 7	Polyunsaturated Fat (g) : 0.6
Sodium (mg) : 154	Cholesterol (mg) : 1

Greek Honey and Lemon Cake
Makes: 16 Slices

This cake is fresh tasting and the lemon flavor just explodes in your mouth. A perennial favourite of lemon fans and of my family. Since it disappears so fast, I always make a double batch. This light cake goes well with a cup of tea or coffee.

Wet Ingredients :

½ cup skimmed milk
½ cup buttermilk
2 tbs. soft margarine or canola oil
½ cup honey
¼ cup fresh lemon juice
2 tbs. freshly grated lemon rind
3 egg-whites, **well beaten (to be added last)**

Dry ingredients :

½ cup cake or pastry flour
1 cup cream of wheat (semolina)
1 tbs. baking powder
½ tsp. ground nutmeg

For topping : 1 tbs. toasted sesame seeds (for topping)

For final glaze : 2 tbs.**each** honey, lemon juice **&** warm water

- Preheat oven to 375^0 F. Lightly grease a 9-inch nonstick cake pan.
- In a medium-size bowl, combine the wet ingredients, **except beaten egg whites.** Set aside.
- In a large bowl, combine the dry ingredients. Add in the wet mixture and gently blend until well combined and free of lumps. **Finally, fold in the egg-whites. Do not overmix.**
- Spoon mixture into prepared cake pan. Sprinkle with toasted sesame seeds.
- Bake for 35-40 minutes or until golden. Take the cake pan out of the oven.

To Glaze the cake:

- In a small bowl, combine the glaze ingredients.
- Spread the glaze over the warm cake, piercing here and there with a toothpick to let in the glaze.
- When all the syrup has been absorbed by the cake, cut into wedges or thin fingers and serve at room temperature.

Analysis per Serving:	
Calories (Kcal) :121.9	Total Fat (g) / % : 2.3 / 16.4 %
Carbohydrate (g) : 23.5	Saturated Fat (g) : 0.2
Dietary Fiber (g) : 0.6	Monounsaturated Fat (g) : 1.1
Protein (g) : 2.8	Polyunsaturated Fat (g) : 0.7
Sodium (mg) : 92	Cholesterol (mg) :0

Spicy Russian Cake   Serves : 10

The aroma of the spices linger on in the house for a few hours after the baking. Impress your friends with this recipe. They will assure you that you are the best baker.

Wet Ingredients:
¾ cup unsweetened applesauce
1 cup frozen orange juice concentrate, brought to room temperature
1 tbs. canola oil

Dry Ingredients:
½ cup unbleached white flour
½ cup whole wheat flour
1 cup cream of wheat
1 tbs. baking powder
1/8 tsp. salt
½ tsp. **each ground** nutmeg, cinnamon **and** cloves
½ cup raisins, soaked in warm water for 10 minutes
3 tbs. chopped walnuts or almonds
½ cup brown sugar or sweetener of your choice

- Preheat oven to 375° F. Lightly grease a 9-inch square, cake pan.
- In a medium-size bowl, combine the wet ingredients.
- In a large bowl, combine the dry ingredients. Gently fold in the wet mixture until well combined and free of lumps. Spoon batter into prepared cake pan.
- Bake for 45 minutes or until top of cake is a beautiful golden color. Cool the cake in the pan on a wire rack for a few minutes, before serving. Tastes best at room temperature.

Analysis per serving :
Calories (Kcal) : 233.5   Total Fat (g) / % : 3.2 / 12.1 %
Carbohydrate (g) : 48   Saturated Fat (g) : 0.2
Dietary Fiber (g) : 2.2   Monounsaturated Fat (g) : 1.1
Protein (g) : 4.8   Polyunsaturated Fat (g) : 1.4
Sodium (mg) : 142   Cholesterol (mg) : 0

Mango Lassi (Mango Milk Shake)   Serves : 6

In India, this milk /yogurt shake is standard fare on the menus in any little deli or restaurant. If you use a blender or food processor, it can be made quickly.

4 cups canned or fresh mango chunks(peeled, if fresh)
Sugar or sweetener of your choice, to taste
1 cup low-fat milk
2 cups nonfat yogurt
1 tsp. ground cardamom
2 cups crushed ice

- In a blender, blend together all the ingredients to a fine consistency like any other milk shake. Serve well chilled.

Analysis per serving:
Calories (Kcal) : 136.1   Total Fat (g) / % : 0.5 / 3.2 %
Carbohydrate (g) : 28.6   Saturated Fat (g) : 0.2
Dietary Fiber (g) : 2.0   Monounsaturated Fat (g) : 0.2
Protein (g) : 6.3   Polyunsaturated Fat (g) : 0.1
Sodium (mg) : 81   Cholesterol (mg) : 2

Lassi Variations

- *The above lassi (milk shake) can be made with other fruits such as pineapple, bananas, kiwis, papayas and peaches.*
- *You can mix your favourite fruits and whip up a lassi easily.*

Meister Muesli   Makes : 19 cups

A treat for anyone looking for a complex-carbo packed start to their day. I came up with this muesli to appease my extremely health conscious husband . Nothing better than to make sure that your first meal of the day is a good one. As for me, I have it as a snack when I feel like doing some chewing exercises !.

4 cups oat flakes
2 cups wheat flakes
2 cups rye flakes
1 tbs. vanilla extract
1 tbs. ground cinnamon
½ cup almonds, dry roasted and cracked (optional)

To be added at the end of the baking:
2 cups grapenuts
4 cups rice Krispies
4 cups cornflakes, low sodium
1 cup raisins, seedless

- Preheat oven to 250°F.
- In a large roast pan or ovenproof pan, combine the oat flakes, wheat flakes, rye flakes, ground cinnamon and vanilla extract. Bake for an hour, turning it every 15 minutes.
- Lower the heat to 200°F. Add the grapenuts, rice crispies, cornflakes, toasted almonds and the raisins. Stir until well combined. Bake for another 15 minutes. Set aside to cool. Store in airtight containers.
- Serve with skimmed milk and fruit of your choice.

Analysis per serving (per cup) : (with almonds)
Calories (Kcal) : 204.7 (226.7)   Total Fat (g) / % : 1 / 4.1 % (3 / 10.9 %)
Carbohydrate (g) : 45.2 (46)   Saturated Fat (g) : 0.1 (0.3)
Dietary Fiber (g) : 7.3 (7.7)   Monounsaturated Fat (g) : 0.1 (1.4)
Protein (g) : 7.8 (8.5)   Polyunsaturated Fat (g) : 0.3 (0.8)
Sodium (mg) : 248 (248)   Cholesterol (mg) : 0 (0)

Mexican Apple & Cheddar Cake

Serves: 12

This aromatic, mouth watering, filling and unique cake is a hearty one, especially for those of you who love to splurge. I, personally, love it with nonfat frozen vanilla yogurt.

Dry ingredients:
1 ½ cups yellow cornmeal
½ cup cream of wheat
1 tsp. ground cinnamon
1 tbs. baking powder
½ tsp. baking soda
¼ tsp. salt

Wet ingredients:
1 ¼ cups skim milk
1 tsp. vinegar
2 cups canned, cream-style corn
3 egg-whites, well beaten
½ cup honey or sweetener of your choice
1 cup shredded low-fat cheddar cheese

For Layering:
2 medium tart apples, cored and thinly sliced, lengthwise
2 tbs. maple syrup
¼ tsp. ground cinnamon

- Preheat oven to 400°F. Lightly grease a 10-inch springform pan.
- In a large bowl, combine the dry ingredients.
- In a medium sized bowl, combine the wet ingredients. Fold the wet mixture into the dry mixture and stir until combined. Spread ½ the batter in the prepared springform pan. Arrange 1/2 the sliced apples overlapping each other to cover the batter. Sprinkle a bit of the cinnamon over the apple layer.
- Spoon in the remaining batter. Arrange the remaining apple slices overlapping each other to cover the batter. Sprinkle the remaining cinnamon. Drizzle the maple syrup over the arranged apples.
- Bake 45 to 50 minutes or until golden brown.

138

- Remove from the oven. Cool in pan or on a wire rack.
- Serve warm, cut into wedges as is or or topped with nonfat frozen yogurt.

Analysis per serving:
Calories (Kcal) : 225.3
Carbohydrate (g) : 46
Dietary Fiber (g) : 2.8
Protein (g) :7.1
Sodium (mg) : 396

Total Fat (g) / % : 1.4/ 5.6 %
Saturated Fat (g) : 0.6
Monounsaturated Fat (g) : 0.3
Polyunsaturated Fat (g) : 0.2
Cholesterol (mg) : 2

Agar-Agar Fruit Mold   Serves: 10

This light, refreshing and irresistible dessert can be whipped up the day before you serve it, for it to set real solid. Agar-Agar is the vegetarian equivalent of gelatin. It is used in South-East Asian recipes, especially in desserts. If you are like me, you'll find it extremely difficult to resist tasting it before the other family members try it.

4 cups peaches or any canned fruits in syrup,
                              juice drained and reserved
1¼ cups water
5 tbs.agar-agar powder or 1 cup agar-agar strips
½ cup sugar or sweetener of your choice
1 cup nonfat yogurt cheese
cooking spray
2 cups each frozen or fresh strawberry

- Add enough warm water to the reserved juice from the canned fruits to make 1 ½ cups of liquid. Sprinkle agar-agar. Stir and let sit for 5 minutes.
- Boil 1 ¼ cups water. Add sugar. Stir. Let the syrup come to boil. When sugar has melted add the prepared agar-agar mixture. Stir. Remove from heat and let cool slightly. When cool to touch, puree canned fruits and cottage cheese together with the cooled agar-agar mix. Fold in the berries at the very end of the process.
- Spray mold in which you wish to set the fruit / agar-agar mixture. Pour the prepared agar-agar / fruit mixture into mold. Chill for 4 hours or more, until well set.
- Serve as is or with nonfat frozen yogurt.

Analysis per serving:	
Calories (Kcal) : 103.7	Total Fat (g) / % : 0.3(2 %)
Carbohydrate (g) : 25.3	Saturated Fat (g) : 0.1
Dietary Fiber (g) : 0.7	Monounsaturated Fat (g) : 0.1
Protein (g) : 1.9	Polyunsaturated Fat (g) : 0.1
Sodium (mg) : 23	Cholesterol (mg) : 0

Pal Paysam (Rice Pudding)   Serves: 4 - 6

Everytime I teach my students how to prepare this pudding of East-Indian origin, I enjoy watching their expressions of euphoria. The Mmm Mmm's tell me what a super hit it is. Some of them make a whole recipe and end up eating it themselves (talk of aerobics for the mouth). Arborio rice gives the pudding a creamy texture. I prefer to make this recipe in the microwave oven, as it needs to be stirred only a couple of times. **This is not a thick pudding. It will get thick as it cools down.**

2 cups skimmed milk
1 can 2% evaporated milk
6 strands of saffron * *
1/4 cup arborio rice

To be added last:
1/4 cup sugar or to taste
1/4 tsp. ground cardamom * *
2 tbs. broken cashews, dry roasted (optional - For garnish)

- In a large, heavy bottomed saucepan combine the milk, evaporated milk, saffron and arborio rice, **on medium-high heat,** Bring it to a boil, stirring occasionally, to keep milk from burning. Lower the heat to medium. Cook until rice is soft to the touch (about 1 hour). The pudding needs to be stirred every now and then to keep the milk from scorching and the rice from sticking to the bottom.
- Stir in the sugar and ground cardamom and continue cooking on low heat, stirring occasionally, for another 10 minutes, or until the sugar has melted and the rice is completely soft.
- **Before serving** : Add the toasted cashews. Serve hot or well chilled .

Analysis per serving (with cashews) :

Calories (Kcal) : 188.8 (212.. 2)	Total Fat (g) / % : 4 / 18.9 % (5.9 / 25 %)
Carbohydrate (g) : 31.1 (32.2)	Saturated Fat (g) : 2.4 (2.8)
Dietary Fiber (g) : 0 (0.2)	Monounsaturated Fat (g) : 1.2 (2.4)
Protein (g) : 7.3 (7.9)	Polyunsaturated Fat (g) : 0.1 (0.5)
Sodium (mg) : 101 (102)	Cholesterol (mg) : 15 (15)

Note :

**Cardamom and saffron give this pudding its wonderful aroma. If you are using these spices for the first time, try using a pinch and work your way up. You can find cardamom and saffron at any East-Indian grocery store or health food store.

Microwave method to make Rice Pudding
(easier because the milk will not burn)

Except for the sugar, combine the ingredients in a microwave ovenproof casserole. Cook on high power, uncovered, for 20 minutes, stirring once in between. Cook on medium power for 25 minutes or until rice is soft. Add sugar and cook for 5 minutes. Add the cashews last just before serving (to retain their crunchiness).

Semia Payasam (Noodle Pudding) :

Instead of the 1/4 cup arborio rice that the recipe calls for, you can substitute 1 cup broken sphagettini that have been lightly roasted in a few drops of butter. Cooking instructions are the same except that the cooking time is considerably less for the noodle pudding , about 20 minutes.

Foccacia (Italian Flat Bread)   Serves : 8

This Italian favourite of many gourmet cooks and "moi" is not as daunting as it is made out to be. This version of the foccacia is easy and the topping can be made as interesting as you want it to be. I usually make it with finely sliced red onions, tomatoes and pineapples (my favourite) and with a garnish of fresh basil and oregano.

2 tsp. active dry yeast
1 tsp. brown sugar
1/2 cup lukewarm water [110°F)
3/4 to 1 cup warm water
1 tsp. dried, crushed rosemary
2 tsp. thymol seeds *(see page 13 for explanation)
2 tsp. salt,or to taste
3 cups unbleached white flour
1 tbs. olive oil
Olive oil for greasing pan
Garnish: 1/2 cup firm, diced tomatoes,
              1/2 cup fresh or canned pineapples, diced
Spices for garnishing : Crushed black pepper and coarse salt to taste
Herbs for garnishing : 1 tbs. fresh **or** 1/2 tsp. **each** fresh basil,
                                       oregano & thyme

- In a small bowl, dissolve yeast and sugar in 1/2 cup lukewarm water. Stir. Let the mixture rest for 10 minutes or until foamy.
- Mix the prepared yeast, rosemary, thymol seeds, salt and flour to make a soft, sticky, yet pliable dough.
- Set aside in a greased bowl. Cover and let rise in a warm place until doubled, about one hour.
- Preheat the oven to 400°F.
- Punch down the dough. Knead and transfer it to a greased 12-inch baking sheet. Leave knuckle impressions on the flattened dough. Brush with olive oil and arrange the sliced onions, diced tomatoes and pineapple to cover the flattened dough. Follow with the spices, the final topping being the herbs.
- Let the dough rise, undisturbed for another 30 minutes.
- Bake in a preheated oven at 400° F for 25-30 minutes or until golden. Serve warm as an appetizer, cut into 1-inch squares or with Pasta E Fagioli for a meal.

Analysis per serving :
Calories (Kcal) : 192.9

Carbohydrate (g) : 37.2

Dietary Fiber (g) : 0.4

Protein (g) : 5.3

Sodium (mg) : 202

Total Fat (g) / % : 2.2 / 10.6 %

Saturated Fat (g) : 0.3

Monounsaturated Fat (g) : 1.3

Polyunsaturated Fat (g) : 0.4

Cholesterol (mg) : 0

Notes : Foccacia dough - Variations

Pizza dough: To make a low-fat pizza dough with your favourite topping, use the foccacia dough recipe + 1/2 cup of flour to make it less sticky. Let it rise and then make your pizza.

White Pizza : Before baking the above pizza dough. Spread the dough to desired size, drizzle 2 tsp. olive oil, sliced red pepper, 2 tbs. of grated parmesan cheese, a few diced tomatoes, freshly crushed black pepper and Italian seasoning, to taste. Bake the white pizza to a light golden brown.

Pizza with Zahtar topping : Just before you bake the pizza dough sprinkle 2 tbs. Zahtar topping and drizzle a tsp. of olive oil and a few thinly sliced onions for a quick, tasty snack.

Zahtar recipe (of North African origin):

1/4 cup sesame seeds
2 tbs. sumac
2 tbs. powdered dry thyme

- Dry roast the sesame seeds in a deep skillet over medium heat for a few minutes, stirring occasionally.
- Allow to cool, then mix with the sumac and thyme. Stored in an airtight jar the blend will keep for 3-4 months.

Fiesta Coffee Cake   Serves : 12

A highly recommended recipe by 100% of my students. My family and I love it with a cup of freshly brewed coffee. For me, its the next best thing to heaven - in desserts. In our home, this cake disappears effortlessly, and the first time I baked it there was nothing left for others to try. So beware !

Wet ingredients:
1 cup non-fat yogurt
1 tbs. vanilla extract
4 ripe bananas, mashed
1 tbs. canola oil
1 tbs. grated fresh lemon peel
3/4 cup brown sugar or 3/4 cup honey or sweetener of your choice
To be added last: 4 egg whites, well beaten

Dry ingredients:
1 cup whole wheat flour
1 cup unbleached white flour
1 cup cream of wheat
2 tbs. chopped walnuts, dry toasted (**optional**)
1 tbs. baking powder
1 tsp. baking soda
1 tsp. **each** ground cinnamon, ground cloves & ground allspice

Glaze:
3 tbs. unsweetened cocoa
1/2 tsp. cinnamon
4 tbs. warm skim milk
2 tbs. honey

- Preheat oven to 375^0 F.
- Lightly grease a 12-inch springform pan.
- In a large bowl, combine the wet ingredients, except egg-whites.
- In another medium sized bowl, combine the dry ingredients thoroughly. Add the prepared wet mixture and combine the two. When well combined, gently fold in the egg whites. Pour batter into

the prepared pan.
- Bake 35-40 minutes or until done. Remove from oven let cool in pan for a few minutes.
- Combine glaze ingredients in a small bowl. When the cake is still slightly warm, spread on the prepared glaze.
- Cut into desired shape and serve with a cup of coffee or tea.

Analysis per serving: (with walnuts)	
Calories (Kcal) : 238.1(246)	Total Fat (g) / % : 2.1 / 7.7 % (2.9 / 10.0 %)
Carbohydrate (g) : 50.2 (50.3)	Saturated Fat (g) : 0.4 (0.4)
Dietary Fiber (g) : 3.4 (3.5)	Monounsaturated Fat (g) : 0.8 (1)
Protein (g) : 7.1 (7.4)	Polyunsaturated Fat (g) : 0.5 (1)
Sodium (mg) : 133 (133)	Cholesterol (mg) : 0 (0)

Index - General

Index

Index - By Cuisine

Index

This book may become a valuable resource if you are interested in healthy lifestyles. "Ultra low-fat" cooking and eating, plus regular exercise are important methods which may enable you to maintain a healthier body weight. This collection of recipes proves that choosing lower fat fare does not have to mean endless salads, tasteless foods, or a deprived diet.

Ron Ward, M.Sc., Clinic Coordinator
Behavioral Medicine Clinic, McMaster University

The students at "The Barn School of Cooking" always find Usha fun and informative and her food colourful, enticing, and <u>delicious</u>.

Teresa Makarewicz,
Professional Home Economist, The Barn Fruit Markets.

Usha Meister is an artist in the kitchen and the classroom. She consistently astounds her students with this artistry by transforming tired standard dishes into brilliant low-fat vegetarian masterpieces. Usha's vast knowledge and charisma makes learning healthy international cuisine both easy and enjoyable. With this book you too can become a student of Usha, the guru of, high quality, low-fat, vegetarian cooking.

Susan Bowinkelman
Program Manager, Continuing Education,Mohawk College

In the course of testing, analyzing and tasting these recipes I found that one could indulge guilt-free. They are easy to prepare, low-fat, heart-healthy dishes. All the recipes taste as good as they look, if not better. This cookbook is a trend setter in healthy eating. This is an exciting alternative cookbook sure to please both gourmets and gourmands.

Marilu Disanto
Nutrition Consultant

This recipe book will provide you with a wide variety of interesting, unusual and exotic tastes, not to mention food that is healthy, satisfying and beautiful to look at. It has been with great pleasure that I have tasted Usha's recipes over the years at many social gatherings, as she experimented with, developed and perfected her dishes, well suited to many palates and diets. Rarely do you find someone devoted to providing us with recipes that are out of the ordinary, yet still healthy and easy to prepare, as well as appealing to a wide variety of tastes.

Donna Scher Ph.D.
Psychologist, Toronto

Dear Reader,

Thank you so much for your support in making my dream, "Usha Meister's Vegetarian Kitchen", a reality. The recipes, I share with you, are those that my students, friends and fans love and that, I, make on a regular basis for our daily meals and get togethers and which have met with consistent accolades.

I would love to keep in touch with you. Should you have any suggestions do drop me a line to the address mentioned below.

Usha Meister's "School of Vegetarian Cooking"
220 West 16th Street
Hamilton, Ontario L9C 4C6

With love and thanks

Usha Meister

Notes